The Art of Pilotage

Also by John Mellor:

The Motor Cruising Manual
Boathandling Under Power
Sailing Can Be Simple
Cruising – Safe and Simple
The Sailing Cruiser Manual
Rules of the Road

and contributions to:

The Best of Sail Cruising
The Best of Sail Navigation

The Art of Pilotage

JOHN MELLOR

SHERIDAN HOUSE

To my father and mother:
who put me on the right course

First Published in the United States of
America 1990 by
Sheridan House Inc.
145 Palisade Street
Dobbs Ferry, NY 10522

The following illustrations are
reproduced by kind permission:
W. S. Amos: Photos 13 and 15
Hydrographer of the Navy: Figures 3,
    17–20, 45, 49, 64, 68–70, 72–74, 79,
    80, 96 and 97
Kelvin Hughes: Photo 28
Macmillan Press: Figures 23, 61, 104
    and 105
Thomas Reed Publications Ltd: Figure 7

ISBN 0 924486 04 X

Printed in Great Britain

Contents

1
The Nature of Pilotage

Pilotage is the specialised business of navigating in inshore waters, and the techniques involved vary in several respects from those employed in off-shore navigation. The basic reason for this lies in the different requirements of the two forms of navigation. When offshore, the navigator is generally in safe open water and what he requires to know is his precise position, so that he can steer accurately to his destination. Close inshore, however, he is usually surrounded by dangers of many kinds – rocks, shallow water, land, shipping lanes, tidal overfalls, and so on – and his most important requirement is, in fact, to know exactly where he is *not*.

This is more logical than it sounds. In such circumstances the navigator can usually see roughly where he is, but very often will not have time to check this position accurately by fixing. He is, however, unlikely to get lost, having already made his landfall, and can check his precise position when time permits, or upon arrival at his destination. Meanwhile he must keep his vessel clear of dangers, so the need to know with certainty that he is *not* in dangerous water is usually more important than the need to know precisely where he actually *is*.

Conventional plotting and fixing is of little use for this as it is both too slow and insufficiently definite in its accuracy. This latter comment means that however accurate a fix may be, it can never place a boat with sufficient certainty for a navigator to pass confidently very close to dangers, as he may have to when piloting inshore. Many of the pilotage techniques explained in this book will, while not giving an actual position, do exactly that.

Not all will, but another aspect of inshore pilotage in small boats has to be considered: because of the speed at which events often occur in such conditions, much pilotage must be done by eye from the tiller, as the skipper may not have time even to glance at a chart, never mind go below to the chart table to peruse one. Many of the most useful techniques can thus be carried out without having to keep constantly referring to a chart.

Much of the secret of successful pilotage lies in such preparation, that on entering pilotage waters the navigator has memorised sufficient details from the charts and pilot books that he can proceed with a clear picture of the area in his mind, much as he would when entering a familiar harbour of which he has 'local knowledge'.

Photo 1 *Piloting close inshore can keep the navigator very busy at times, with so much going on around him.*

Notwithstanding all this, there will still be times on a coasting passage when the skipper will use more conventional forms of navigation, such as running a dead reckoning plot and shooting fixes. Although you, the reader, are assumed to have a basic understanding of conventional navigation, the particular ways in which it is used in pilotage waters are covered in the early part of the book.

Finally, it is tempting to think that, with electronic navigation systems such as Decca, Loran and Satnav that give a skipper a continuous and accurate readout of his position at all times in all weathers, much of the contents of this book are outmoded. Apart from the fact that much of the book deals with the conduct of the pilot rather than with simply finding the boat's position, only a crass idiot would charge around the coasts totally reliant on a little black box of electronics (see chapter 14). Traditional, reliable systems of position fixing and pilotage will remain, certainly in the foreseeable future, essential tools for the competent navigator.

2
Entering Pilotage Waters

Things happen much more quickly in inshore waters than they do offshore, and there are many more dangers to contend with. It is most important that both the boat and the prospective navigation are thoroughly prepared beforehand if all is to go smoothly. The seamanship and navigation aspects of sailing a boat are rather more closely linked when she is traversing pilotage waters than they are when she is out in deep water, so both will be considered here.

Pilotage waters can, of course, be entered from two directions – seaward and landward. The preparations discussed in this chapter apply not only to boats entering coastal waters after a sea passage, but also to those slipping from a mooring in a river or leaving a coastal marina.

Initial preparations for pilotage work should be made well in advance of entering the waters for which it will be required. Much must be memorised, and it should be done far enough ahead of being needed to allow it to be gently and thoroughly assimilated into the brain. A maths master at school once told me that the best preparation for an important exam was to go off for a totally relaxing week's holiday. His theory was

that if you revise right up to the day of the exam, then the last thing memorised will sit firmly on top of the brain and blanket all the rest. Time is needed for the mind to digest all the information properly so that each bit of it can be readily retrieved when required. The same thinking applies to memorising information needed for entering pilotage waters.

Charts and Books

Charts of suitable scales should be carried to cover passagemaking (small scale), coastal cruising and landfall (medium scale), and harbour approaches (large scale); also a Tidal Stream Atlas and Pilot Book of the cruising area, and an Almanac. Charts and Pilot Books should also cover any harbours you may have to dodge into for shelter. All charts, Pilot Books and Almanacs should be corrected to date each winter from 'Notices to Mariners' or published correction services; or returned to the local chart agent for correction.

A logbook must be maintained at all times as it enables you to store a mass of useful information on weather and navigation. An hourly entry of weath-

---

Fig 1 **NAVIGATION EQUIPMENT**

Charts	Echo-sounder
Parallel Ruler	Binoculars (7×50)
Dividers (one-handed)	Hand-bearing Compass
Compasses	Steering Compass
Pencils (2B)	Log
Pencil Sharpener	Leadline
Rubber	Nautical Almanac
Clock	Pilot Books
Radio with Long Wave (for	Tidal Stream Atlases
Shipping Forecasts)	Navigator's Notebook
Barometer	Deck Log

---

er conditions, course steered, estimated leeway, distance run and so on should be recorded, along with all information on course alterations, fixes, etc; each entry being accompanied by log reading and time: see later section in this chapter. Figure 1 gives a checklist of essential navigation equipment.

A small navigator's notebook, which can be slipped into an oilskin pocket, will be found extremely useful for keeping brief notes when entering harbour etc (see later section).

Navigation Equipment

Both steering and hand-bearing compasses should be carried on board. The steering compass should be checked and adjusted by swinging every other year, or after major work on the boat that might affect it. This job should be done by a professional compass adjuster.

A leadline is absolutely essential for inshore pilotage, and it should have a hollow in the base for 'arming' with tallow, lard, grease or something that will pick up a sample of the seabed. Checking the nature of the seabed against what the chart says it should be is a very useful, if old-fashioned technique for assessing your position, particularly in thick weather.

An echo-sounder is particularly convenient as it saves having a crew member casting the lead all day. It also gives you a continuous readout of the depth, which is especially helpful when following or seeking out a particular depth contour. An echo-sounder with deep and shallow water alarms makes this process even simpler.

A log to record distance run through the water is most important as this

Photo 2 *Thorough preparation at the chart table is essential before entering pilotage waters. Fancy equipment is not necessary; the traditional tools shown are simple, reliable and perfectly adequate.*

Photo 3 *An echo-sounder is probably the most useful of all electronic gadgets in pilotage waters. This one has shallow and deep water alarms that can be set to warn of crossing depth contours.*

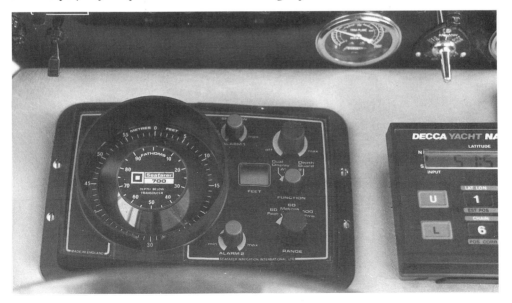

is a very difficult thing to assess, even with long practice. It should be checked periodically over a known distance without tidal stream influence, so as to ascertain its accuracy. If you find a fixed error this must be noted in the logbook for application to all readings. A handy standby, should the log fail you, is the Dutchman's Log. This, in essence, consists of throwing something over the bow and timing how long it takes for you to sail past it. You can then calculate quite easily, from the length of your boat and the time taken, your speed through the water. Much time and possible miscalculation can be saved by working out beforehand a selection of speeds and times for your boat, so that you can simply read off from the time the speed you are doing (see figure 2).

A stopwatch will be found most useful, not only for timing a Dutchman's Log, but more importantly for timing the characteristics of lights on lighthouses and buoys. In certain situations these can be very confusing and the more accurately you can time them the better.

Binoculars are almost essential for pilotage work as they enable you to identify features accurately at much greater ranges than the eyes; 7x50 is the type you should have, having satisfactory magnification with good light-gathering power for use at dusk. Anything more powerful will be very difficult to hold steady.

An accurate clock, barometer and radio with Long Wave for shipping forecasts will enable you to keep track of the weather situation, which is a great deal more important close inshore than it is out at sea. With the proximity of land and all the other dangers along a coast (see chapter 7) the skipper in pilotage waters cannot simply heave to and go to sleep if things get nasty, as he can out at sea.

Fig 2 DUTCHMAN'S LOG

1 knot = 6000 feet in 3600 seconds

$$= 1\tfrac{2}{3} \text{ ft/sec}$$

1 ft/sec = $\tfrac{3}{5}$ knot

From this we can calculate the formula $S=3L/5t$ where $S=$ speed in knots; $L=$ length in feet; $t=$ time taken in seconds

For a 30 foot yacht $S=18/t$ and this can be tabulated as follows:

Speed	Time
½	36
1	18
1½	12
2	9
2½	7.2
3	6
3½	5
4	4.5
4½	4
5	3.6

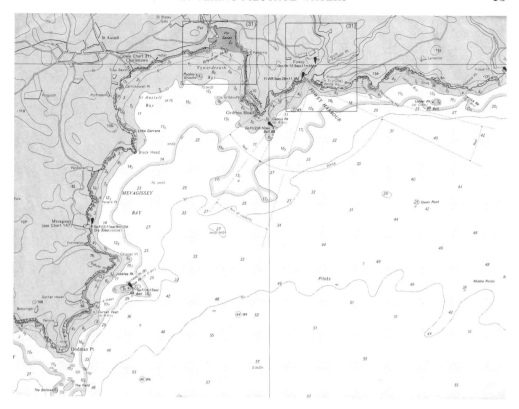

Reading the Chart

There is a considerable amount of detail on a chart, presenting the navigator with vast quantities of information that he must understand how to interpret (see figure 3). *Admiralty Chart Booklet 5011* lists all the symbols used on Admiralty charts together with their meanings. Most proprietary yachtsman's charts use very similar symbols, although they tend to be less cryptic than the Admiralty ones, giving more detailed information actually on the chart.

It is essential that a pilot be able to glance briefly at a chart and interpret accurately what he sees. Very often there simply will not be time to search booklets and almanacs for explanations, so you must learn thoroughly all the symbols and the precise meanings of

Fig 3 Details of scale, depth measurement units, position of Chart Datum, information on surveys, etc, are noted by the title. Latest corrections are noted in bottom margin. The numbered squares indicate the coverage of large scale harbour charts of that number. As here, a number of harbours are often included on one chart.

light characteristics, charted heights and depths, and so on. There is neither space for, nor point in listing all the symbols here, but in figure 4 you will find the more important interpretations and definitions.

Converting the vertical plan on the chart to the horizontal view that you will see from the cockpit takes some skill and experience. However, a few useful guidelines will help.

By and large, many objects that look prominent on the chart will not be so when viewed from the boat, and vice versa. A massive beacon two miles – some three kilometres – high will be shown on the chart as a dot inside a small circle, perhaps barely noticeable amongst a mass of trees and houses. From a boat approaching the coast, however, you will see it long before anything else on the chart comes up over the horizon. On the other hand a very distinctive-looking harbour break-water may be a couple of feet only above a spring high water and quite invisible from the boat against a background sea wall.

You should always check the charted heights of objects, and assess the heights of features for which no height is given, before deciding what will be seen from a particular vantage point. Even tall objects may be lost behind high office blocks when viewed from certain angles. The nature of the background is also important insofar as it may absorb the feature you are looking for, or make it stand out more clearly than you would expect. Headlands, for example, will often blend into one another when viewed from along the coast, while small buoys may stand out far more clearly against pale cliffs than they do against the sea and the sky.

This business of identifying features will be discussed more fully in chapter 3.

Buoyage Systems

Although navigation buoys can be unreliable in terms of position, and even existence at times, due to the possibility of them dragging their moorings, especially on coasts exposed to bad weather and strong tidal streams, they play a major role in coastal and harbour pilot-

---

Fig 4   CHART DEFINITIONS

Depths	are measured	*below CHART DATUM*
Drying heights	are measured	*above CHART DATUM*
Tidal heights	are measured	*above CHART DATUM*
Shore heights	are measured	*above MEAN HIGH WATER SPRINGS*
Bridge clearances	are measured	*above MEAN HIGH WATER SPRINGS*

Units used in these measurements are given below the chart title

Bearings are noted in degrees (True) as viewed from seaward (Transits, arcs of lights, etc)

Ranges of lights are in nautical miles assuming 10nm visibility and no height of eye limitation on horizon distance

Colouring on Admiralty Metric charts

BUFF	=	land
GREEN	=	drying area between High and Low Water
BLUE	=	area inside 5 metre depth contour
BLUE LINE	=	marks 10 metre depth contour

Photo 4 *A port-hand buoy of the Lateral system. Note even number, can shape, light and radar reflector. The lattice-work reduces wind resistance but maintains the shape, especially at a distance.*

age. There are two main international buoyage systems; the lateral system for marking the sides of channels, and the cardinal system for marking the safe sides of dangers. Certain areas, such as North America, utilise quite different systems in some specific areas, such as inland waterways, and the local Pilot Books should be studied carefully for details. Full details of major systems are given in Appendix 1.

In theory, the position of a buoy should first be fixed before using it for navigation. In practice, in a small boat, you should take care to check as well as you can the positions of buoys before relying on them. Generally, buoys in the approaches to large commercial harbours will be well-maintained and watched, so should prove fairly reliable. Others, particularly in remote, stormy or tide-strewn areas of coastline, must be treated with caution. Such buoys, especially home-made ones in small creeks, may also be so rusty, battered or covered in bird droppings as to be almost unrecognisable. Cardinal buoys may even take on quite different meanings to those intended, if their topmarks have been bashed off by passing coasters and colour schemes altered by the droppings of cormorants.

Withys (sometimes topped by baked bean tins), beer barrels, old plastic diesel cans and the like will often be met with in the nether reaches of rivers and creeks. Pilot Books may describe these places as 'marked with buoys' or 'channel marked with withys', but in truth it can often be very difficult in a winding creek to decide which side of the channel the mark is on – assuming that when you get there someone has not taken a few home for repainting. You will find some guidance on these problems in chapter 11.

Preparing the Boat

Before entering pilotage waters you should thoroughly check and prepare the boat for all possible eventualities, bearing in mind that events may happen quickly and there might not be sufficient time to check, organise or look for things when you get involved in your close quarters navigation.

Make all your normal engine checks – oil, fuel, batteries, etc – then run up the engine to warm it through, to ensure that it starts, and to check that nothing is amiss. Check that the gears engage properly, that oil pressure and water temperature are correct, and that cooling water is being ejected satisfactorily. You will then feel confident that all will be well should you require the engine urgently. If the batteries are low, then continue running the engine to charge them right up in case you need power for lights, VHF, searchlight and so on.

Check that the windlass is working properly and that the anchor and cable are ready to be cleared away quickly for possible hurried use on entering the restricted waters. Check operation of the VHF with a radio check call to a nearby vessel or coast radio station. Check your navigation lights, chart table light, searchlight, torches, etc if you will be approaching in darkness, and check your horn. If you have an aerosol type, and it feels nearly empty, then change to a new one; you do not want it to run out right in the middle of a busy harbour when manoeuvring signals are urgently required.

Check that the echo-sounder works properly and that the leadline is conveniently available. Check through your chart folio to ensure that you have the requisite larger scale charts for the waters you are about to enter, and

that the local Pilot Book and Almanac are where they should be by the chart table. Clean all old plotting off the charts, then stow them in the folio in the order in which they will be needed. Check all your chart equipment – pencils, rubber, dividers, parallel rule, etc – and the hand-bearing compass. The accuracy of the latter can be confirmed by comparing its reading when aligned with the fore-and-aft line of the boat with that of the main steering compass (corrected for deviation). Make sure you hold it in a place known to be free of deviation.

In figure 5 you will find a checklist for all the items that should be prepared before entering pilotage waters.

Preparing the Approach

Much of 'local knowledge' is simply recognising the general layout of a harbour, estuary or coastline, and being able to identify for certain the salient features. These are the things that you should concentrate on memorising. More detailed aspects of an entry into pilotage waters – such as tidal heights and times, etc – can and should be noted in a navigator's notebook for quick reference (see next section). It is best not to clog the brain with too much information of the type that can be readily ascertained from a quick glance at the notebook.

With the chart in front of you, read carefully through the Pilot Book for the area, cross-checking information with that on the chart as you go. Check for unexpected tidal effects – eddies, slack areas, and so on – and note transits, leading marks, prominent features, etc, and see where and how all these tie in with the details on the chart. Note places where large conglomerations of

```
┌──────────────────────────────────────────────────────────────┐
│                   Fig 5  PREPARING THE BOAT                    │
│                                                                │
│ Engine oil level                                               │
│ Engine coolant level                                           │
│ Engine seacock filter                                          │
│ Gearbox oil level                                              │
│ Reduction box oil level                                        │
│ Sterntube greaser level                                        │
│ Fuel tank level                                                │
│ Run engine and check: gears, throttle, oil pressure,           │
│ cooling water, charging, temperature, etc                      │
│ Anchor windlass operation and chain clear to run               │
│ Torches                                                        │
│ VHF radio (do not call Coastguard for radio check)             │
│ Echo sounder                                                   │
│ Leadline                                                       │
│ Radar (if fitted and not in use)                               │
└──────────────────────────────────────────────────────────────┘
```

moorings might hinder what appears on the chart to be a clear passage or anchorage area.

Inspect closely the surrounding land contours, woods, large tracts of buildings and so on, and try to gain a general impression of what it will all look like from the low horizontal viewpoint of your cockpit. This is not always easy, especially as your viewpoint will be altering constantly during the approach. It is important to learn how to convert the vertical view on the chart to the horizontal one from your boat, and it requires some concentration and thought. Generally you should appreciate the fact that conspicuous-looking features on the chart – breakwaters, headlands, and such – will not be so when seen from low down to seaward. High hills, large trees, tall buildings, and so on, will not look very obvious on the chart unless their heights are given and carefully compared with that of the surrounding land, but they will be most conspicuous to you.

A night-time approach requires particular care. Those conspicuously-marked leading lights may in reality disappear completely in the general blaze of background lighting from pubs, discos, promenade lights, and so on. The general glow of shore lights in the sky may not be the seaside port you are seeking but a large industrial town miles inland from it. Beware also the lights of cars passing gaps in buildings, which can sometimes give the distinct impression of flashing or occulting red or white harbour lights. I was nearly caught out by this once when approaching Naples, the timing of car rear-lights passing a gap being absolutely identical, when checked over a period, to the leading light we were seeking.

Try to foresee possible difficulties like

these, then you are forewarned if they do occur on closer approach. Look for as many supporting features as you can find to help check the basic approach marks that you will be using. A clear picture of the general layout of things can be a tremendous help in giving early warning of uncertainty. If the overall appearance of the approach does not seem right according to your studies, however clear and certain the approach marks appear to be, you should heave to and check out all the possible guides to your position before proceeding. This saved me from considerable embarrassment once when entering Dartmouth, happily steering on a red light in a restaurant window instead of on the second leading light. Even at night, the general shape and position of the surrounding land and the big Mewstone Rock outside made it clear that we were not on the right track.

Checking the Route

When you have a reasonable picture in your mind of the general layout of the area, work along your protracted route on the chart, mentally noting buoys, beacons, transits and other marks that will help you keep track of position or enable you to keep clear of dangers. Check carefully the positions of all dangers, and that your proposed course passes through clear water all the way. At this stage do not bother to write details in the notebook; just endeavour to gain a general picture of the overall area and of your basic plan for entering or negotiating it. Then leave it all for a while and have a cup of tea while it settles in your mind. Later, go back and repeat the whole process, and do so until you are thoroughly confident that you know and can visualise the area, and your passage through it, as well as

you possibly can. Then you can take up your notebook and start making more detailed plans.

The Navigator's Notebook

In here should go no more than the bare bones of your plan; just the complex details that you may forget and want to refer to rapidly. Enter the times and heights of high and low waters covering the period of the passage, and the height of tide for each hour in between. If you are passing a number of ports, then do this for each one and clearly indicate which port the information is for. If you are taking tidal stream information from the diamonds on the chart (see chapter 4) then this also can be listed with direction and speed for each hour against each diamond. A brief note of the position on the chart of each diamond will also save time. Use either latitude and longitude or a range and bearing from a prominent feature. With a Tidal Stream Atlas you can simply pencil in the times and dates on each page of the atlas for quick reference.

You should also list the details of buoys, transits, etc, that you will pass or that mark places where you need to alter course; the courses you should alter to, and so on (see figure 6). A simple sketch plan of the entry to a harbour, and particularly the final approach to a berth, will be found most useful.

Keeping the Deck Log

This is an essential piece of equipment for coastal pilotage as, if properly kept up, it can provide you with masses of useful navigational information, such as times of fixes, course alterations and so on. If anything should happen to the chart you should be able to go to the deck log and reconstruct from the infor-

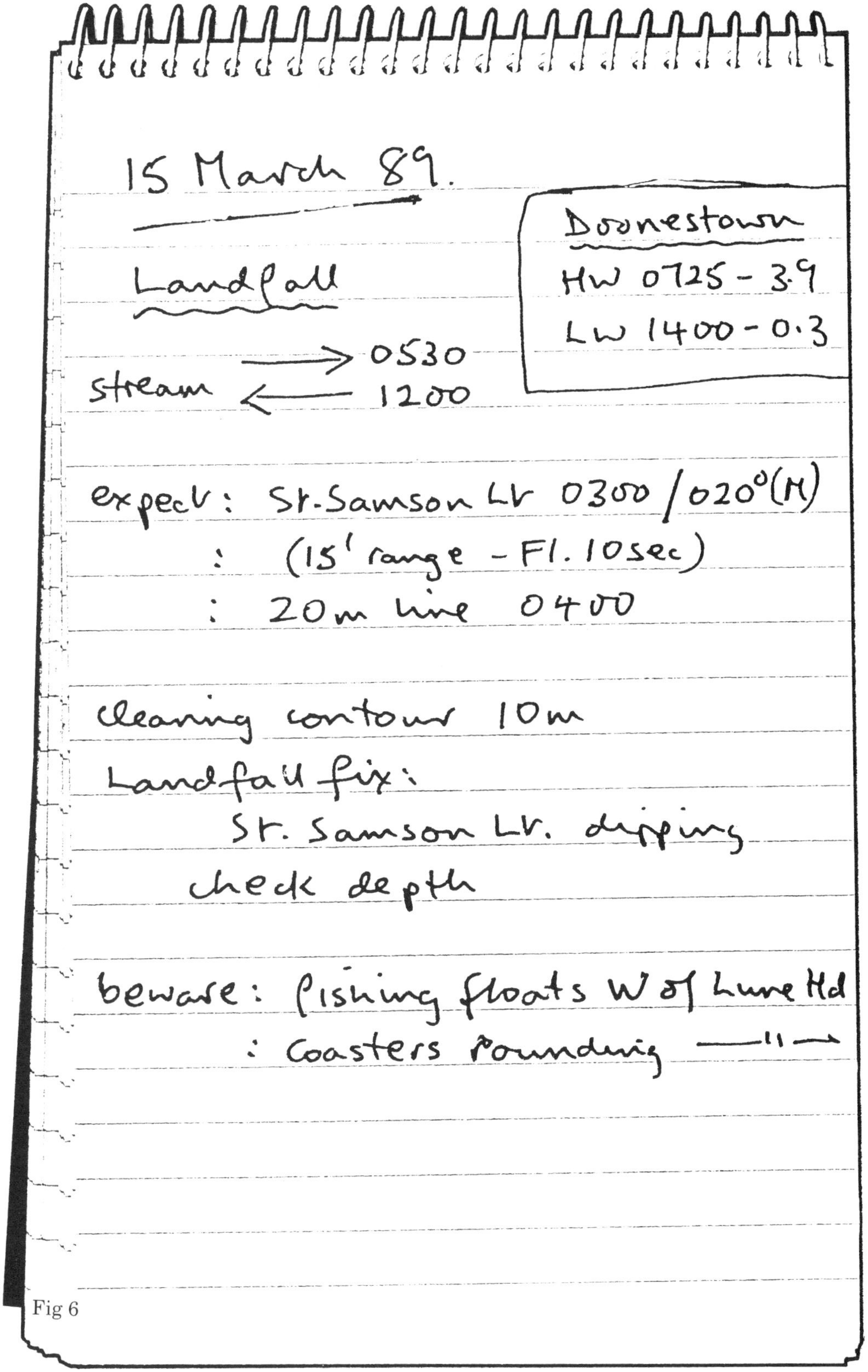

15 March 89.

Landfall

stream   → 0530
          ← 1200

Doonestown
HW 0725 - 3.9
LW 1400 - 0.3

expect: St. Samson Lt 0300 / 020° (M)
     : (15' range - Fl. 10 sec)
     : 20m line 0400

clearing contour 10m

Landfall fix:
    St. Samson Lt. dipping
    check depth

beware: fishing floats W of Lune Hd
     : Coasters pounding ——''——

Fig 6

mation in it all details of your passage to date. In principle we can say that all projected plans should go into the navigator's notebook and all completed plans into the deck log. The navigator's notebook should help you to go where you intend, while the deck log should contain all details of where you have been to date.

Figure 7 shows a sample page from a good deck log. Note the regular details of course steered, leeway, helmsman's error and log reading. These, together with the details of course changes with times and log readings, and full details of all fixes, should enable you to plot your track and calculate current position at any time. In the hurly-burly of coastal pilotage you may not find the time to plot regularly on the chart, but with this information in the log you will be able to go back in a quieter moment and put it all together.

This does not, of course, absolve you from plotting on the chart, as clearly the logbook does not show dangers to navigation, etc. For all the short cuts and time-saving dodges that will be discussed in this book, nevertheless the keeping of a constant, up-to-date and accurate plot on the chart is absolutely essential.

The logbook should also enable you to keep track of the weather. Regular entries of barometer readings, wind strength and direction, together with a note of general weather conditions and sea state, will help greatly in your interpretations of shipping forecasts and the development of the actual weather in your area.

Keeping a Lookout

It may seem rather obvious to state that a good lookout is absolutely essential when negotiating pilotage waters, but there are several reasons for it which

Fig 7

DATE Tues 10th June 19..... LOG OF YACHT Lundy

FROM Rosslare / TO Falmouth / AT Barnstaple Bay

	Dover	Milford Haven	
H.W.	04h. 02 min	11h. 11 min	
L.W.	11h. 14 min	17h. 23 min	
H.W.	16h. 25 min	23h. 35 min	
L.W.	23h. 45 min	— —	

TIDAL STREAMS at Lundy turn W'ly at 0323. E'ly at 0901.
at Hartland turn WSW. at 1510. ENE at 2112.

1 HOURS	2 COURSE by COMPASS	3 Error	4 Deviation	5 Distance by Log	5a Distance in Hours	6a WIND Direction	6b WIND Force	6c Leeway	7a TIDAL STREAM Direction and Rate Knots	7b TIDAL STREAM Allowance	8 Barom'r / Therm'r	9	10
0 (Midnight)	⚓												
1 (a.m.)	in Rosslare												
2	"												
3	"												
4/50	Various	12°	1°N	0		S	3-4		225°-1	10°	1026 / 16.1°		
5	167°	"	"			"	"		225°-2	20°			
6	167°	"	"	18		"	4		225°-2	20°	1024 / 16.7°		
7	167°	"	"			"	"		225°-2	20°			
8	189°	11°	1°W	36		SxW	5	3°	180°-2	0°	1023 / 17.8°		
9	143°	"	"			"	"	"	180°-1	6°			
10/20	149°	"	"	52		"	"	"	SLACK	0°	1019 / 18.3°		
11	154°	"	"			"	"	"	030°-1	8°			
12 (Noon)	150°	"	"	66		SSW	5	3°	000°-1	4°	1016 / 19.4°		
13 (1 p.m.)	153°	"	"			"	"	"	350°-2	7°			
14 (2 p.m.)	148°	"	"	78		SSW	6	5°	330°-2	0°	1013 / 20°		
15 (3 p.m.)	148°	"	"			"	"	"	SLACK	0°			
16 (4 p.m.)	142°	10°	1°W	90		"	"	"	225°-½	5°	1009 / 20°		
17 (5 p.m.)	137°	"	"			"	"		225°-1	10°			
18/05 (6 p.m.)	147°	"	"	101		SWxS	6	5°	SLACK	0°	1008 / 18.3°		
19 (7 p.m.)	133°	"	"			"			030°-1	8°			
20 (8 p.m.)	147°	"	"	112		SW	7	10°	040°-2	17°	1008 / 17.2°		
21 (9 p.m.)	⚓					"	"	"	040°-3	25°			
22 (10 p.m.)						SW	6				1007 / 16.7°		
23 (11 p.m.)													
24 (12 p.m.) (Midnight)						W	5-6				1007 / 13.3°		

DAILY REMARKS

CREW

At anchor in Rosslare Harbour.

4.10 Hove up anchor. 4.10 Rounded Rosslare Breakwater.
4.30 Whistle By close abeam to port. Set Log at Zero.
4.40 Tuskar Rock abm. 1M. to starboard. Log 3. A/C. 175° True for Longships (126 Miles)
6.30 Sea moderately rough when clear of land. Set steadying canvas.
8.30 Fresh breeze. Fine and clear. Moderately rough sea and W'ly swell. Vessel rolling easily.
9.00 Wind & sea increasing with falling barometer so decided to run up the Bristol Channel & anchor in Barnstaple Bay. A/C. 135°T. - direct to Smalls Lt. Ho.
10.00 Sighted Smalls Lt. Ho. on port bow.
10.20 Smalls Lt. Ho. 3M. to port (by vert. sextant angle.) Log 54½ A/C. to 132°T to bring Hartland Pt. right ahead.
12.00 Fresh breeze. Rough sea. Overcast. Vessel labouring.

Weather threatening. Glass still falling; wind steady.

16.30 Strong breeze. Vessel rolling and pitching violently at times. Overcast and clear.
16.50 Sighted Lundy Island on port bow.
18.05 Lundy Island N. Pt. abm. to port 9M. (By cross bearings). Log 101½ A/C. 110°T. to leave Hartland Pt. 1M. to starboard.

20.00 Moderate gale. Squally. Overcast & clear. Vessel labouring to rough sea and swell.
20.12 Hartland Pt. abm. 2M. to starboard. Log 113½. A/C. 135°T.
20.30 Vessel in shelter of coast. Took in steadying canvas.
20.40 Clovelly Pier abm. A/C to starboard to bring it right ahead. Approached coast using echo sounder.
20.45 Anchored in 5 fathoms. Took anchor bearings and exhibited anchor light. At anchor in Clovelly Roads. Strong breeze. Slight sea.

Day's run 110 Nautical Miles
Time under way 16 h. 40 min
Average speed 6.6 knots

Engine started 04 05
Engine stopped 20 45
Engine running 16 h. 40 min

	FUEL – GALLONS/LITRES	FRESH WATER
On Hand	300	100
Received	—	—
Total	300	100
Consumed	30	10
Remaining	270	90

ANCHOR BEARINGS

may not immediately spring to mind. It is not the keeping of a lookout as such that matters, but what the lookout sees and registers as important.

Collision avoidance in the often congested coastal waters clearly requires a good lookout, and the sorts of shipping problems facing the lookout are discussed in detail in chapter 12. Keeping a lookout for the navigator, however, bears investigation, as there are certain simple techniques which can help greatly in both seeing and identifying navigation marks from a distance.

The general principle of keeping a lookout should be to regularly sweep slowly right round the horizon with the naked eye, then with the binoculars, then have a rest. If you spot something very faint, especially at night, you will generally find it easier to see clearly in the corner of the eye if you look slight-

ly to one side of it rather than stare at it directly. This is something to do with the structure of the eye's cones and rods making peripheral vision more efficient than direct vision.

At night your eyes will adjust automatically to the darkness, the pupils opening wider so as to admit more light and increase what you can see. This 'night vision', as it is called, takes some twenty minutes to reach maximum efficiency after your eyes have been exposed to white light, so it is imperative that a lookout avoids such exposure. Chart table and galley lights should be red at sea, as light of this colour has much less effect on night vision. Spreader lights should be used only in harbour or in dire emergency.

Special lookout techniques are required in poor visibility and these are discussed in chapter 10.

3
Making a Landfall

This is the beginning of your pilotage and if it is not accurate then practically every word of advice in the rest of this book will be a waste of time. Clearly the accuracy of your landfall depends in principle on the accuracy of your offshore navigation to date. However, there are several ways in which any previous uncertainty in your navigation can be salvaged, and an accurate landfall made, even if your position on approaching pilotage waters is in doubt.

Unless weather conditions make a specific and accurate landfall essential – running for shelter from a gale for example (see end of chapter) – it is important to appreciate the benefits of arriving at the wrong place and knowing for certain that you are there, as opposed to arriving at the right place and only thinking you are there. This is not gobbledygook, merely pragmatic navigation. If you know exactly where you are, then it is a relatively simple matter to proceed to where you should be; if you only know vaguely that you are somewhere near where you should be, then how do you get there?

The simple way round this problem is to make your landfall at a place where you can be certain of getting a good fix, which may not necessarily be at your destination (see figure 8). You can then, with a reliable position on the chart, safely alter course towards your destination.

If this is not possible, due either to a featureless coastline with no suitable fixing places, or to a very unreliable position on approaching the coast, then you must modify this technique somewhat.

The Offset Landfall

One simple way of rescuing a dubious landfall is deliberately to aim off so far to one side of your destination that there can be no doubt which way it lies when you raise the coast. In principle you then alter course in that direction and proceed with hope in your heart until you find it (see figure 9). You must assess as carefully as you can your maximum possible error in position, add a good safety margin and then set course to make landfall this distance to one side of your destination.

This could also apply to the finding of a harbour entrance lost in a mass of houses or lights; if you approach well to one side of the town you will then know for certain which way to turn to find the harbour – meantime perhaps using a depth contour to keep in safe water.

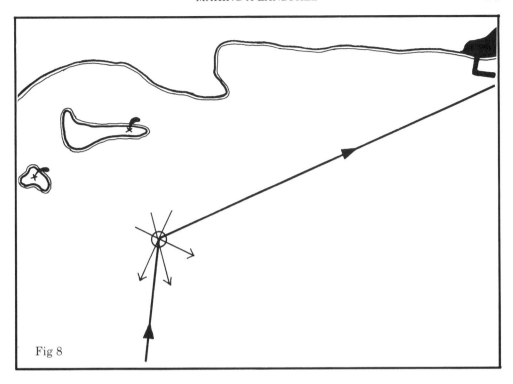

Fig 8

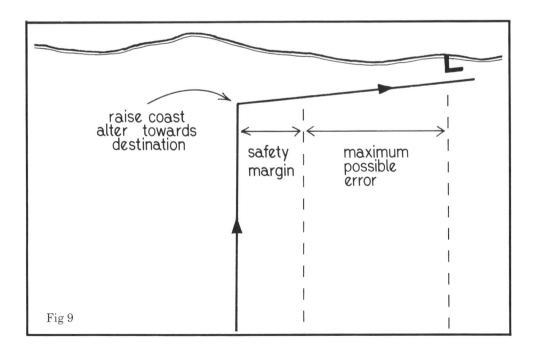

raise coast
alter towards
destination

safety
margin

maximum
possible
error

Fig 9

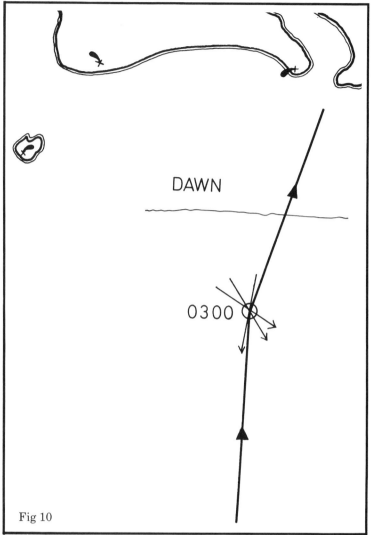

Fig 10

Another common situation is slightly different in that it does not necessarily involve an anticipated poor landfall. When approaching a coast with fierce tides, particularly in light winds, gales or poor visibility, it would be very wise to aim deliberately for a landfall up-tide of your destination just in case you get set down-tide in the final approach.

Landfall at Night

On many coasts there is much to be said for arranging a landfall in dark-ness, when coastal lights often provide an easier and more accurate landfall fix than can be obtained in daylight. If the landfall is made just before dawn this benefit can be followed by closing the coast and negotiating the pilotage waters in the light. With the vessel's position accurately fixed, daylight will be found generally to give easier conditions for tricky pilotage, when the navigator will be looking for a variety of clearing lines, and often at the general appearance of the water, to find the way to his destination (see figure 10).

Circumstances, of course, will vary, and a badly-lit coastline should not generally be approached at night unless other features such as depth contours enable safe water to be maintained. If the vessel's progress cannot safely or conveniently be slowed in order to delay landfall until first light, then the prudent skipper will either alter course to make a landfall further along the coast where lights will give him an accurate fix, or (if conditions permit) he will heave to in a depth of water that he knows to be safe, to await daylight.

Landfall in Fog

This requires very careful consideration and handling, and will frequently call for a landfall deliberately offset so that the vessel approaches a part of the coast endowed with suitable depth contours that will enable the skipper to both keep clear of dangers and also to work towards an accurate fix. This topic is discussed fully in chapter 10.

Timing the Landfall

To a certain extent this has been covered in previous sections, but many factors make a landfall easier at some times than at others. When approaching a coast with off-lying sandbanks, for example, it is often far easier both to keep safe from them and to check your position when the tide is low enough either to expose the banks completely, or at least to cause the seas to break clearly and distinctly around their edges (see chapters 4 and 7). Strong wind-over-tide conditions may blur the demarcation of these breakers from the normal seas and you may find that they show much more clearly if you wait until the tide is running with the wind. The same thinking applies in rocky areas that have

isolated half-tide rocks and reefs.

On a less precise note, it may be worth delaying an arrival off a harbour that is difficult to see until the local fishing fleet either departs or returns. I do not suggest that you follow local fishing boats, as they very often enter a harbour by idiosyncratic routes that for various reasons might not suit you. They will, however, show you the general approach and the position of the entrance if these are not clear.

The Landfall Fix

This is, in principle, no different from any other kind of fix, but it has certain psychological aspects that are worth considering. The first is that it is very tempting to get one on the chart as soon as possible, and it is all too easy to knock off a totally inaccurate fix the moment the first mountain peeps over the horizon – when you still may be twenty miles from the nearest danger. There is no need for this. On the other hand, the gradually unfolding features as you slowly close the coast will certainly enable you to build up a picture in your mind of the general appearance of things. You can then, as was discussed in chapter 2, consider how it all ties in with your prepared mental image of the landfall.

At the same time, if there is any likelihood of a poor landfall, then the sooner an accurate fix is on the chart the better. You then have maximum time to adjust your course to the correct landfall with the least amount of detour – which could be very important if you are closing a lee shore in any strength of wind, or are approaching a coastline with very strong tidal streams.

A most useful initial landfall fix can often be had at night by crossing the dipping range of a powerful light with

Photo 5 *Cranes are not usually marked on charts but they can be seen at considerable distances, and often provide a valuable guide to the position of a large commercial port.*

its compass bearing (see chapter 6). In suitable conditions of clear visibility with low cloud you may be able to get a bearing and an approximate guess of the range from the loom of a big light, or even the loom of town lights ashore. This latter needs to be used with caution, however, as distant inland cities often show up far more clearly than coastal towns and harbours.

Funnelling your Fixes

There are a number of useful guides to making the landfall that can give approximate indications of your position while still some way off the coast. These can tell you whether you are on the right general track or not, and prepare you for the increasingly accurate series of fixes that you will be able to make as

the coast comes steadily nearer.

The presence of shipping, whether in designated shipping lanes or simply congregating to round a distant headland, can be a helpful guide. The course that these ships are steering can often indicate which side of a headland you are approaching, and the sizes of the ships can tell you whether you are approaching a major shipping lane or an inshore route for coasters.

High ground inland will be seen generally at considerable ranges in clear weather, and a close inspection of the nether regions of the chart can indicate which part of the coast you are heading for. Mountains can even give a very rough fix, but you need to be aware of the difficulties in identifying them.

As you gradually approach closer to the coast, you should be able to utilise such position lines as depth contours, RDF bearings and so on, to plot rough fixes which you can compare with your dead reckoning plot (see chapter 5). If the fix and the EP are in the same general area then it is likely that you are on the right track. If they are not, then you must do some urgent re-checking of both fix and EP.

If you find everything disagreeing wildly, and the coast is inhospitable, then you should consider heaving to and awaiting better conditions (night, perhaps, with clearly identifiable shore lights; or daylight, if the coast is not well lit), or the arrival of a passing ship which can furnish you with a position. Bear in mind, however, that even commercial ships can produce some very dubious positions at times.

All being well you will be able to improve steadily the accuracy of your plotted position until you reach the situation where you can safely and reliably identify sufficient features to obtain a good and accurate landfall fix. From this position you can then proceed confidently into the wilds of the pilotage waters ahead.

Identifying Navigation Marks

The correct identification of buoys, lighthouses, prominent shore features, and so on, is clearly crucial to the accuracy of your landfall, and also to that of the ensuing pilotage to your destination. There is always a dangerous tendency, especially on making landfall, to assume that the feature you see is the one you expect to see. A rather cursory check is then all too often made on the identification, resulting in the wrong thing being apparently identified as the right one. This inclination must be strenuously resisted and even the most apparently obvious lighthouse checked and double-checked most carefully before deciding on its identification.

Another major problem is caused by the fact that many features that seem prominent on the chart are actually not so when seen from the boat, and vice versa. Low breakwaters, for example, stand out very clearly on a chart but can blend imperceptibly into the background coastline when viewed from the boat. Beacons that appear most insignificant, being marked simply with a blob and *Bn*, may sometimes be massive structures visible for miles. Trees marked (conspic) may be found far less so than a neighbouring one that has grown recently.

It is important to realise how much extra information is to be found in the Pilot Book than is marked on the chart. There will often be very useful photographs, that can help to resolve the problem of headlands, for example. Careful study of the book will show up such things as apparently insignificant beacons, etc, as complete descriptions of them will be given. The daytime appearance of lighthouses will be described in detail (perhaps even drawn or photographed), as will conspicuous trees, buildings, and so on. It takes some experience to interpret these things properly on a chart and the Pilot Book is a very useful adjunct.

Separating Headlands

Headlands can be particularly difficult to identify with certainty. When viewed from offshore they tend to blend into the background coastline completely. When viewed from along the coast, the headland that looks prominent on the chart often appears less significant than a slight bump along the side of it facing you. It is all too easy to take a bearing of the bulge instead of the main head-

Photo 6 *It takes experience to identify with certainty the shore features as you approach land. Take every opportunity to compare the chart with known coastlines when you are sailing in familiar waters.*

land, and think that the main headland is actually the next one along the coast. Even if a lighthouse sits on the headland the blending of the tones, especially in slightly hazy weather, can cause the same mistake. Headlands need to be identified with great care. It helps if you can assess from the chart how steeply the end of it drops into the sea, but this is not always easy either.

Characteristics of Lights

Identifying the characteristics of lights would seem to be a straightforward matter, especially as those in close proximity to one another have quite different characteristics. In rough weather, however, when boat or buoy (or both) are heaving up and down on the waves, the light will be obscured much of the time. It can then be very difficult to time accurately, and can even, over a period, appear to be exhibiting a quite different characteristic to its true one. In situations like this especially you must time the light over as many periods as possible, using a stopwatch for accuracy. Then check neighbouring lights also to ensure that they all tie in with the overall light pattern of the coastline.

You should also check carefully the

quoted range of a lighthouse (see chapter 2) against its range from your EP, taking into account the distance at which you would expect to see it pop over the horizon according to your height of eye. A low-powered light, especially in slightly hazy conditions, may well not be sighted until long after its dipping range. A powerful light, on the other hand, may well show its loom on low clouds at much greater ranges than its dipping range.

Identifying Buoys

Buoys can be particularly difficult to identify when you are faced with a winking mass of them in the approaches to a large harbour. Variations in intensity can cause far ones to appear close and near ones to seem distant. Coloured lights always seem fainter, and thus further away than white ones; and lights that you think of as being distant, due to being around a bend in the channel, may in fact be nearer as the crow flies, and thus brighter than the one you are heading for.

It can help greatly when trying to sort out a mass of buoys to plot a line on the chart from your position in the direction you are looking, then try to visualise how all the nearby buoys lie in relation to this line and to one another. Look for buoys that lie nearly in transit with others or with shore lights or anchored ships, etc; these may be obscured or overpowered by the objects or lights in line with them. Select the buoys from the chart that you are most concerned with and try to pick out only these, ignoring the others to begin with. You then can widen your view gradually to the other visible lights and slowly build up a picture of what you see ahead. The identification of all the relevant lights will then become a good deal easier.

The Electronic Landfall

This, of course, is the easiest landfall of all, and it is tempting to think that suitable electronics will make all comments about night and fog and suchlike obsolete. The skipper so equipped should, however, always consider the possibility of electronic breakdown. If possible his landfalls should be made according to the traditional rules, using his electronics to produce simple and accurate fixes along the way, but always keeping navigational options open, so that he can work his way out of trouble if the electronics fail. A blind passage totally dependent on electronic fixing, during which there is no way to continue safely, or reliably to escape into clear water or a temporary haven if they pack up, is asking for trouble (see chapter 14).

Running for Shelter

As will become apparent when the difficulties of accurate landfall are considered together with the dangers to be encountered close inshore (see chapter 7), this can be a very hazardous occupation requiring considerable forethought and careful planning. A well-found vessel with a competent crew is seldom in serious danger out in open water, in even the worst of gales. The same vessel running down onto a lee shore in search of shelter, however, could most easily be lost with all hands if the slightest navigation or seamanship miscalculation is made, or a very minor gear malfunction experienced. In my view there has to be an extremely good reason indeed for a boat to throw away the safety of a good offing at sea for the very risky alternative of a run for shelter.

Having said that, the type of pilotage conditions awaiting the skipper at the end of the run will have a consider-

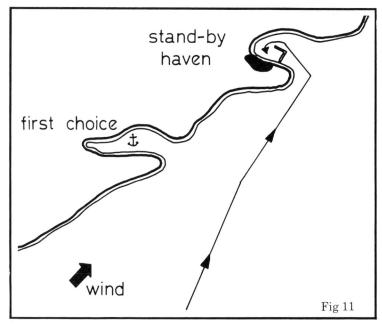

first choice

stand-by
haven

wind

Fig 11

able effect on the level of risk involved. With a suitable place to run to, and proper precautions taken, the risk can be reduced greatly if sufficient reason exists to justify a run for shelter. Such reasons might be a serious and worsening leak in a wooden boat's seams, illness in a crewman, or something similar.

Safe Havens

The best possible situation to run to for shelter can be seen in figure 11. Here we have a shore that is not directly downwind, so that a reasonable boat should be able to sail clear of it if necessary, without having to go hard on the wind. The skipper's first choice of harbour is totally sheltered with a wide, clear entry that will give progressively calmer water during the final approach, as the boat comes increasingly onto the wind. If he makes landfall to weather of the harbour he can easily run down to it without having to gybe. If he makes landfall to leeward of it he has a stand-

by harbour that he can run down into instead.

Dangerous Havens

In contrast, figures 12 and 13 show two types of harbour that would be extremely dangerous to run for in a rising onshore gale. The shallow bar across the entrance in figure 12 would cause steep, high breaking seas, especially on the ebb, that could broach and overwhelm any boat trying to cross it for the protection beyond. Even if the bar is sheltered from the direct effect of the wind, a long swell will run round the corner and break on it just the same (see chapters 7 and 9). The other harbour, fairly typical of the English East Coast, is narrow, protrudes into possibly a strong cross-tidal stream, and is fronted by shallow water. The seas off and around this entrance would be steep and very confused, making the accurate steering necessary for negotiating the narrow entrance extremely difficult (see chapter 7). There would be a strong

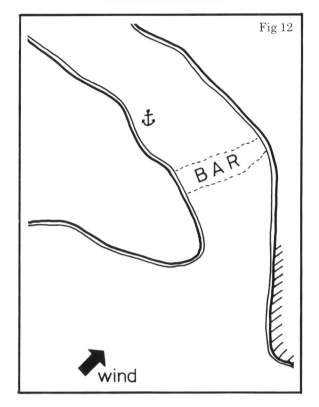

Fig 12

BAR

wind

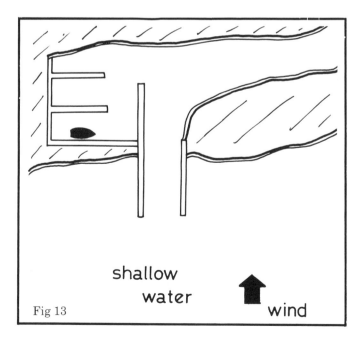

shallow
water wind

Fig 13

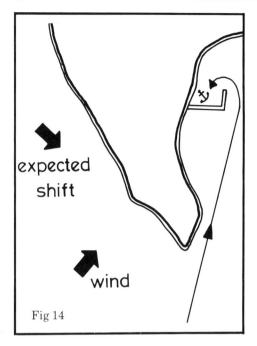 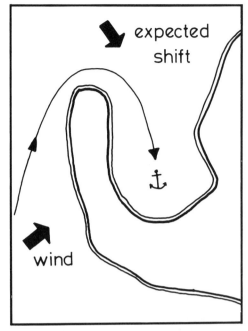

Fig 14

likelihood of landing up sideways across one of the pierheads, followed by almost certain loss of the boat, and possibly of the crew.

Changing Conditions

Even if the landfall and entry are good, as in figure 11, it is important to bear in mind the possibility of the wind shifting and continuing to blow hard. If running for shelter from a sou'west gale caused by a depression to the north, for example, it would be wise to ensure that the haven also provides shelter through west right up to north. It is by no means unknown for such a sou'west gale to shift nor'west on the passage of a vicious cold front and then blow even harder. Compare the two havens shown in figure 14.

4
Tides and Tidal Streams

Tides, and the accompanying streams caused by them, are of paramount importance to the coastal navigator or pilot. To the navigator of a small sailing yacht or low-powered motor cruiser, tidal streams dictate virtually every move, especially in areas such as the Channel Islands where they run very strongly. It is absolutely essential that a coastal pilot has a thorough and complete understanding of their behaviour if he is to make competent passages and safe landfalls.

It is not only in negotiating harbours and anchorages that tidal height is important. Many coastal areas have shallow and drying banks that can be traversed perfectly safely at certain states of the tide, but not at others. A skipper can often save himself much time or discomfort by knowing when he can pass through these shallows, as they can provide him with both short cuts and also shelter in certain situations, as well as enabling him to avoid the full strength of foul tides (see chapters 7 and 13).

The Behaviour of Tides

Tides are caused by the gravitational pull of the sun and the moon, the moon's pull being the stronger. Spring tides occur once a fortnight, around the full and new moons, when sun and moon are pulling together in line. This strong pull generates a large range of tide, producing high High Waters and low Low Waters. Between the spring tides – when sun and moon pull at right angles – we have neap tides, with much smaller ranges than the springs.

Although we refer to spring and neap tides, the range actually changes constantly, from a maximum at 'top of springs' (about two days after the full and new moons) to a minimum at 'dead neaps' (about two days after the moon's first and last quarters). It does not, however, change steadily, but rather staggers along somewhat like a drunk negotiating steps, two forward and one back. For example, in each 24-hour period as the range is making up towards spring tides, it will increase in height one tide then decrease a little on the next, before making up properly the next day. There is also a fortnightly hiccup in the system; the full moon springs having greater range than those at new moon, and the first quarter neaps having less range than those of the last quarter. In other words, the full moon produces bigger springs than the new

moon, and the first quarter slacker neaps than the last. These timings and variations are somewhat approximate, but a study of your local Tide Table should make the general pattern clear.

These variations are not mere academic frippery; they are of considerable importance when grounding or drying out. You cannot assume, for example, that if you get into a berth on a full moon spring tide that you will necessarily get out again on the next new moon spring – and so on. Springs, incidentally, always occur at about the same time for any particular place, and neaps will be six hours different.

Geographical influences can cause tidal ranges to vary from virtually zero in some places to around 50ft in others. This is because the tide travels like a wave, and this wave is affected by shallow water, reflection, refraction, etc, just as a sea wave is. In some places

Photo 7 *At Low Water a wide river can often shrink to a narrow trickle of a channel, or even dry out altogether.*

it stays low and in others it is pushed up high (see chapter 7). The direction in which this tidal 'wave' flows along a coast can be seen clearly from the way the slack water area travels along on a Tidal Stream Atlas during the flood, and also from the steadily changing time of High Water at ports along a coast. Almanacs and Pilot Books will often show charts indicating these directions of flow, and the places where different tidal flows meet.

Calculating Tidal Heights

High and Low Water times and heights are tabulated in Tide Tables and Almanacs for selected major harbours.

Those for nearby minor places are calculated by applying adjustments to the tabulated figures for the nearby major one. Different Tide Tables and Almanacs have their own ways of doing this, but generally information is given for each Standard Port, with accompanying corrections for a list of neighbouring secondary ports. Precise details will be given in the relevant publication.

There are two basic methods for calculating the height of the tide at times between High and Low Water: the simple 'twelfths rule' and the more accurate 'graphic method'.

In the vast majority of cases, perfectly sound and workable heights can be calculated mentally in seconds using the twelfths rule, with any amount of approximation to simplify the sums. All the errors in the world that might be generated by this approach will pale into insignificance beside the safety margin that any sensible seaman will routinely apply to all his depth calculations (see later sections).

In certain cases of unconventional tides, such as in the Swanage area on the South Coast of England, special calculations do have to be made, and details will be found in the Almanacs or Tide Tables for such places. Before looking at the abnormalities, however, let us compare the graphic plotting method of finding tidal heights with the sailor's approach. Let us calculate the height of the tide at Mistley Quay on the River Stour in Suffolk at 0915 clock time on 25 July 1987, by both the twelfths rule and by the graphic method in the MacMillan Almanac.

Twelfths Rule

The twelfths rule states quite simply that the tide rises and falls in a reasonably regular manner, accelerating up to

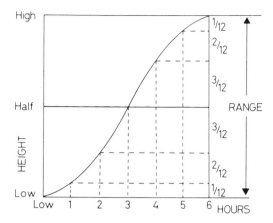

Fig 15

half tide, then levelling off its rate of change before decelerating at the same rate to full tide (high or low, as the case may be). In the first hour it changes by one twelfth of its range (difference between High and Low Water heights); in the second hour by two twelfths and in the third by three twelfths. It then levels, changing by three twelfths again in the fourth hour, two twelfths in the fifth, and one twelfth in the sixth and last hour (see figure 15). It adheres to this pattern at all times – springs, neaps and at all stages in between. Thus all that is needed from the book are the times and heights of High and Low Waters, from which to make all the calculations.

Tidal Heights from Twelfths Rule

The local Tide Tables for Mistley give us Low Water at 0635 (1.04m) and high water at 1308 (3.73m). These figures give us a range of 2.69m; and dividing this by twelve gives one twelfth of the range as about 0.22m. Thus by 0735 the tide will have risen to 1.26m; by 0835 it will be 1.7m, and at 0935 it will be 2.36m. We interpolate for 0915 to give about 2.14m of tide at Mistley Quay. If we continue this calculation to High Water we find a height of 3.68m at 1235, as opposed to the tabulated value of 3.73m at 1308. Working the twelfths rule back from the tabulated High Water gives us about 3.62m for 1238 and 1.7m for 0915. Common sense tells us to calculate from the end of the range nearest to the time required, in which case discrepancies will be no more than a few centimetres. In this example we would work from Low Water, and for all practical purposes we can say that there will be about 2m of tide off Mistley Quay at 0915 clock time on 25 July 1987, according to the twelfths rule (see figure 16).

TWELFTHS RULE

LW	0635	------	1·04m
+1	0735	+1/12 (0·22) =	1·26
+2	0835	+2/12 (0·44) =	1·70
**	0915	------	2·14m
+3	0935	+3/12 (0·66) =	2·36 ·
+4	1035	+3/12 (0·66) =	3·02
+5	1135	+2/12 (0·44) =	3·46
+6	1235	+1/12 (0·22) =	3·68
HW	1308	------	3·73m

Fig 16

In practice, the reality of this calculation for an experienced navigator would go something like: Low Water at half six – one metre; High Water at one o'clock – three and a half metres; range is two and a half metres; a twelfth is 0.2 metres; half seven is 1.2 metres; half eight is 1.6 metres; half nine is 2.2 metres; 0915 is 2 metres. Not only does this kind of simplification reduce considerably the likelihood of calculation errors, but the whole process probably takes less than ten seconds in the skipper's head. Compare the figures with the more accurate ones above.

The Graphic Method

The Admiralty Tide Tables, and certain Almanacs, print a graph alongside each Standard Port, on which is drawn the changing height of the tide during a twenty-four hour period. Usually this approximates very roughly to a sine curve. Finding intermediate heights between High and Low Water involves plotting lines on this graph according to the time required.

Tidal Heights from the Graph

In the Almanac we find that the Standard Port for Mistley is Harwich, and the Harwich Tide Table gives Low Water clock time as 0615 (0.94m) and High Water as 1243 (3.64m). The time differences for Mistley are, from the table in figure 17, +0020 minutes when Low Water is near 0600 or 1800; +0025 minutes for High Water near 0000 or 1200. The height differences are: approx +0.07m for High Water of 3.64m (interpolating between MHWS and MHWN); −0.1m for Low Water of 0.9. Applying these corrections gives us values for Mistley of: Low Water = 0635 (0.84m); High Water = 1308 (3.71m).

Go to the graph in figure 18 and mark the Low Water height along the scale at bottom left, and the High Water height along the scale at top left. With a pencil and ruler plot a line between these two points as shown. Then find the time, along the scale beneath the curve, for which the height of tide is required (either before or after HW; in this case we want fractionally less than four hours before HW), and follow

Fig 17   **Standard Port HARWICH (──►)**

Times				Height (metres)			
HW		LW		MHWS	MHWN	MLWN	MLWS
0000	0600	0000	0600	4.0	3.4	1.1	0.4
1200	1800	1200	1800				

Differences MISTLEY

+0025	+0025	0000	+0020	+0.2	0.0	−0.1	−0.1

NOTE: Harwich is a Standard Port and times and heights of tidal predictions for each day of the year are given below.

Fig 18

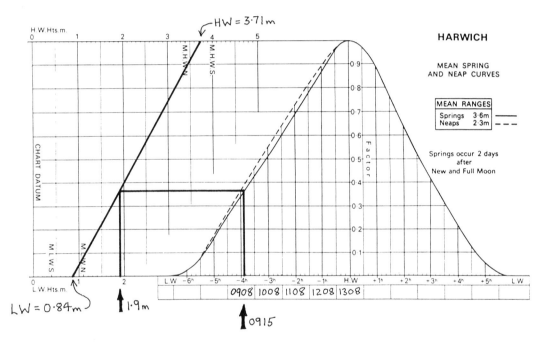

this line vertically up until it meets the curve nearest to the actual state of tide (spring or neap; or interpolate between the two). Then lay a ruler horizontally between this point and the line drawn on the left, and mark where it crosses this line. The height of tide at that time can then be read off from the scale at the top or bottom of this left-hand side of the diagram. In this case there is a value of 1.9m for 0915, as you can see marked.

Comparison of Methods

In this fairly typical example the accurate method gives a value that is three inches less than that calculated mentally in about ten seconds using the twelfths rule. The wash of a passing motorboat will change the water level by more than that (as will a thick pencil line on the graph); and the amount of calculation and plotting involved in this

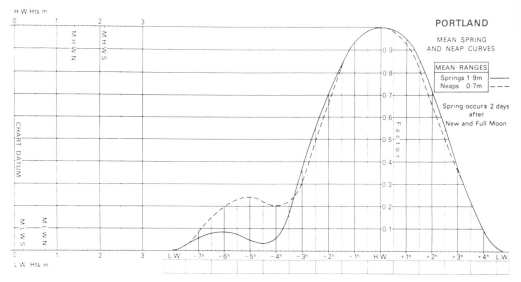

Fig 19

SOUTHAMPTON   10-2-22

Hampshire

CHARTS
   Admiralty 2041, 1905; Stanford 11; Imray C3, Y30; OS 196
TIDES
   HW (1st) −0001 on Dover; ML 2.9; Zone 0 (GMT)

Southampton is a Standard Port and tidal predictions for each day of the year are given below. See Sections 10.2.7 and 10.2.8. A NE gale combined with high barometer may lower sea level by 0.6m. At springs there are two separate HWs about 2 hours apart; at neaps there is a long stand.

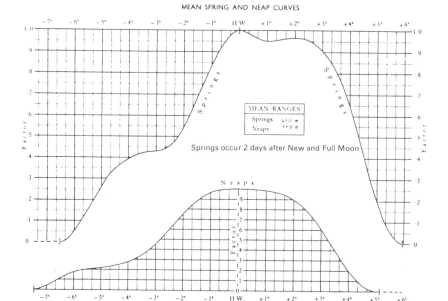

Fig 20 *Note that this chart separates springs and neaps as their curves are different in scale. Note comments at top right; see later section Meteorological Effects on Tides.*

method *must* make it considerably more prone to error when piloting in difficult inshore conditions. However, see next section.

Irregular Tides

Because of geographical restrictions on the flow of the water, some places have very uneven tidal patterns. The irregularity often takes the shape of a long stand at High Water (perhaps as much as four hours) followed by a rapid plummet to Low Water, or even an initial fall for a couple of hours followed by a rise to a second High Water before finally falling to Low Water. The extent of the irregularity will also vary between neaps and springs. This is the sort of pattern experienced in the Solent; while Portland and Weymouth have double Low Waters during spring tides. Other places have irregular rates of rise and fall between High and Low Waters. Compare the tidal curves for Portland and Southampton in figures 19 and 20 with that for Harwich in figure 18. The twelfths rule will not work with such tides, and intermediate heights must be plotted as described in the graphic method above.

Tidal Heights Offshore

The increase in height of the tidal wave on approaching the coast causes tidal ranges in harbours and along the coast to be greater than those further offshore. When calculating a tidal height for an off-lying bank or danger ideally you should use a co-tidal chart. If such a thing is not available then use the nearest port, but apply a good safety margin. Check the times and heights of the tide also for neighbouring ports so that you can assess some sort of average, particularly in terms of the time.

You can usually reckon that a tide will have roughly ¾ of the harbour range a few miles offshore, and ½ the range further out.

Reduction to Soundings

This expression is used to describe the business of subtracting the tidal height from the actual depth of water, in order to find the chart sounding in that place. Reduction to soundings is most important when using an echo-sounder for navigating, as it is the sounding on the chart that provides a position line (usually a depth contour, in fact), not the depth of water the boat is floating in. Figure 21 shows the relationship between tidal heights and soundings. An arbitrary level known as 'chart datum' links the two measurements; tidal height being measured above it, and chart sounding being measured below it. If the seabed rises above the level of chart datum, the sounding is underlined to indicate that the measurement shown is *above* chart datum. These underlined soundings are known as 'drying heights', presumably because those places usually dry out at Low Water spring tides.

To avoid confusion it is important to realise that although chart datum is close to Low Water springs it has no direct connection with it, in terms of its definition. It is an arbitrary level, defined as a level below which the tide rarely falls. It is very close to the lowest astronomical tide (LAT). Some old charts may have a higher chart datum, close to MLWS (Mean Low Water Springs) so the actual depth of water will be slightly less than that calculated if current tidal heights (measured above the CD close to LAT) are added to soundings on such charts (which will be measured below the high-

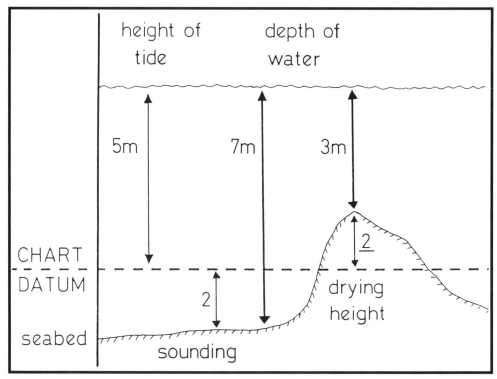

Fig 21

er CD close to MLWS). The position of chart datum used for soundings will be noted under the chart title.

Clearance under Bridges

The heights of bridges are given above Mean High Water Springs (MHWS) so the true clearance beneath them varies with the height of the tide, usually being greater than that marked on the chart – but sometimes less (at equinoctial spring High Water, for example). The height of MHWS above chart datum will be noted on the chart, usually under the title, so the difference between it and the current tidal height can easily be calculated, in order to find the actual height of the bridge above the water at the time.

Meteorological Effects on Tides

Weather conditions can affect the calculated heights and times of tides, sometimes quite dramatically. Tidal heights are predicted for average atmospheric pressure, and any change from this will affect the height; high barometric pressure pushes the tide down lower than predicted, and low pressure allows it to rise higher than expected. As a general guide, a change in pressure of 10 millibars will alter the height of the tide by about 0.1m. It will take a little time before a change in pressure begins to exert this effect.

Strong winds persisting over a period of time can affect the tidal height, raising it in the direction towards which it is blowing, and lowering it in the other direction. This effect increases with the strength and duration of the blow. In certain places where a particular wind direction blows into an enclosed 'dead end', the effect can be exaggerated to the extent of producing what is known as a storm surge, due to the piled-up water having nowhere to go. Northerly gales cause this trouble at the southern end of the North Sea, and predicted heights can be exceeded by as much as two or even three metres. This was the reason for the construction of the Thames Barrage. A side effect of such a surge is that upwind of it the tide is lowered, due to all the water being blown downwind. A further subsidiary effect of strong winds can be to delay the arrival of the tide, thus altering predicted times. These effects are sometimes noted in Pilot Books and Almanacs, as you can see in the top right hand corner of the Southampton tidal curve in figure 20.

It should be apparent that tidal calculations must be used with some caution, and the wise seaman will always bear in mind all the factors that could alter them. He will also appreciate that he may not be aware of everything that might upset his calculations and so will incorporate a comfortable safety margin, in terms of both time and height, at all times.

Tidal Streams

There are two basic sources of information on tidal streams – Tidal Stream Atlases and tidal diamonds on the chart. By and large, the former give a general picture of the tidal stream flow over a wide area of sea, while the latter give detailed, and apparently accurate figures, for individual specific places. There is a distinction here which it is important to understand.

Neither source is totally accurate, nor totally reliable, as there are so many unpredictable factors that can alter the rate and direction of a tidal stream from day to day; mainly wind and atmospheric pressure changing the forecast times and heights of the tide, and thus affecting the flow of the stream. Accepting this, however, we can say that the overall tidal stream information given in a Tidal Stream Atlas is most suitable for use on a passage, while tidal diamonds give more accurate figures for close-quarter pilotage, around sandbanks and harbours, for example; but only in the close vicinity of the diamond.

Tidal streams that flow first one way then the next are called rectilinear streams. They are generally encountered along straight coastlines and through passages between islands. They tend to have a period of slack water at the turn, perhaps as long as an hour or more in places. Rotary streams flow round bays, and a slack water period is not usually experienced.

Rates of Tidal Streams

Tidal streams are, of course, directly affected by the tides. The greater the range of tide the faster the streams will flow, in order to move the larger amount of water in the fixed time of six hours. Spring rates are thus much stronger than those at neaps, and places with large tidal ranges, such as the Bristol Channel or the Channel Islands, will have very much faster stream rates than those with small ranges. The general direction of flood and ebb streams around a coast should be found in an Almanac or the local Pilot Book, and the Pilot Book will also give details of any vagaries in the stream rate or direction caused by local conditions.

The rate of flow of tidal streams is also directly related to the rate of rise and fall of the tide in that place. Thus, except in areas of irregular tides (see above), rough estimates of the rate can be made using, in effect, the twelfths rule. From this we can deduce that the stream steadily accelerates as the tide begins flooding or ebbing and reaches a peak rate at half-tide. It then steadily slows down in proportion, eventually reaching zero when the tide turns.

Tidal Stream Variations

There are many things that can affect the rate and direction of flow of tidal streams. The first important fact to appreciate is that streams outside a harbour or river do not usually coincide with those inside. Very often the stream can continue to flood for three hours or more along the coast after it has begun to ebb from a river. The basic reason for this is that, although that particular river may have filled up with the tide and be ready to empty again, the next one along the coast has not. Thus the coastal tide has to continue flooding until it has.

Photo 8 *The speed and direction of the tidal stream can clearly be seen as it flows past a buoy.*

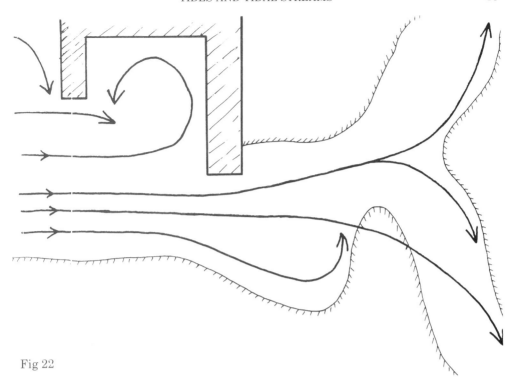

Fig 22

A similar situation occurs in very long tidal rivers, where the flood can continue in the upper reaches for some hours after the ebb has begun down at the entrance. The time taken for the tide to get up the river results in a much later High Water at the head than at the entrance. These variations in timing can often enable a clever skipper to carry favourable tides on a coastal passage for a great deal longer than the expected six hours. Careful study of the Pilot Book can bring useful dividends here (see chapter 13).

Meteorological effects on times and heights of High Water (see above) will also affect the run of the stream, and its rate.

Geographical Effects on Tidal Streams

Physical influences, however, have probably the greatest effect on the expected run of the tidal stream. Generally, streams seek out the path of least resistance, and this means deep water with no obstructions. The main run of the stream will thus be found along the deep channels, with the rate of the stream steadily slackening as it spreads out into the shallows.

The stream will also be reluctant to go round corners, so will be found strongest on the outside of bends where the bank finally forces it to go round. By the same token it will tend to run straight past bays, leaving slack water inside them. It may even hit the far end of the bay and be forced back round the inside in a back eddy, depending on the shape of the bay at its end. In certain places this back eddy can be almost as strong as the main stream, and can be a very useful help to the skipper working against the tide along a coast. Some bays, however, will experience a slight set in along the length, then a similar set out towards the end. The Pilot Book will advise on this sort of behaviour.

The tendency of the stream to go straight on at bends can cause a cross-flow where the bend is between under-water banks rather than river banks, the stream tending to flow out of the bend and over the bank. A similar phenomenon is experienced when the tide is rising and fills up a deep channel. It will then tend to flow out sideways, often quite strongly, over the surrounding banks. The skipper creeping through the shallows in search of slack streams needs to watch for this tendency. On the ebb the stream will flow off the banks into the deep channels.

A similar cross-stream can also occur when the main stream runs past a side channel, particularly when the side channel cuts across a spit to rejoin the main stream on the other side. The stream passing the exit will tend to draw water through the side channel quite strongly. This is quite a common occurrence when islands are dotted about in the main stream (such as in the Hebrides) or when river mouths are extended by drying spits.

Besides slowing down in shallow water, streams can also be accelerated when they are forced to pass through narrow gaps. These gaps are not always obvious, as they can be caused by underwater banks and even opposing streams, as well as by bridges, locks, islands, river banks etc. In figure 22 you can see the general behaviour of streams under geographical influences.

Meeting of Tidal Streams

With all these main streams and subsidiary streams zooming about in different directions and at different strengths there will inevitably be places where they meet. Very serious turbulence can exist in such places, particularly in strong winds at spring tides, and they can pose great dangers to small boats (see chapter 7).

5
Coastwise Dead Reckoning

Dead reckoning consists of keeping track of your progress and position by plotting distance run and course made good. It is a basic technique that can be used for navigating in all situations – coastal, offshore, ocean – but the accuracy required by the coastal pilot is far greater than that required by the offshore navigator who, by and large, uses it to keep general track of his position until he can obtain a landfall fix, astronomical fix or whatever. If he has to go some length of time without a fix it will not upset him greatly as he is unlikely to crash into anything if his DR is a bit out. The coastal navigator, if he cannot get frequent good fixes, is totally reliant on an accurate DR for keeping him out of trouble.

Although much of the time tidal stream effects will be fairly simple on a coastal passage – being ahead or astern generally – it is absolutely essential that accurate calculations of these effects can be made for all directions and durations so that an accurate DR plot can be maintained in all circumstances, particularly in conditions of low visibility. There will certainly be times when cross-tides affect the pilot, such as when crossing estuaries for example, and these are often the times when accurate DR is most necessary.

The principle of running a DR plot is not difficult; you draw a line on the chart from your starting point (departure fix, landfall fix or whatever) in the direction you are steering, then once an hour mark on it the distance you have sailed along that line during the hour, according to the log. To run a DR plot accurately, however, taking into account all the factors that conspire to prevent you following that line at that speed, requires some skill and experience in assessing those factors. Let us look at what prevents a sailing boat from proceeding along her line like a car on a motorway.

Leeway

This is the amount a boat drifts to leeward while sailing along, measured as an angle by which her track through the water differs from the direction in which she is pointing. It is zero when running downwind, and increases steadily the closer you sail to the wind, reaching a maximum when beating. An average cruising boat beating to windward in average conditions can usually reckon to make something in the region of five

Photo 9 *Delightful sailing, but is the helmsman concentrating on his course?*

degrees leeway. This will increase with angle of heel, wind strength, sea state, any tendency to pinch too close to the wind, and any reduction in speed due to poor sail trim, etc. Excessive windage from top-hamper, surplus rigging and so on, or reduced lateral resistance due to small keel area or incorrect hull trim will also increase leeway. A slow cruising boat plodding along under short canvas will make a good deal more than will a hard-sailing racing boat. Precisely how much your boat makes under a variety of conditions is very much a matter for you to judge from experience, and you should make a point of checking it whenever possible. Then when the classic wild, thick night comes along with you trying to make

for shelter, you will *know* what leeway she makes. The above pointers should help.

Helmsman's Error

This is the difference between the course you tell the helmsman to steer and the one he actually does steer. This is not usually due to cussedness, but the simple fact that, especially in a breeze of wind and a bit of sea, it is very difficult for all but the most skilled of helmsmen to actually maintain the course ordered. It is most important for a skipper to watch carefully every helmsman (surreptitiously, so that he does not feel hounded!) in order to judge just how far off the course he is averaging. An experienced helmsman will be able to gauge this for himself and will tell you his error. Helmsman's error is usually greatest while reaching down a big sea, when the boat will tend to gripe into the wind all the time, causing the course made good to be somewhat upwind of that theoretically steered. Upwind error is also often experienced when running dead before a strong wind, when a slightly nervous helmsman is likely to hold up a little for fear of gybing. On the wind a helmsman will often be optimistic about how close he has been sailing, and the true course made good is likely to be downwind of that claimed.

Log Error

This can be caused by the machine itself, by weed on the paddle or impeller, or by weather conditions. Check the first periodically by running a known distance with no tidal stream and note any permanent error. Withdraw and clean impellers regularly, and after sailing though patches of weed. In light weather logs tend to under-read due to friction in the system, and in rough weather over-read, because of the tendency to steer a somewhat zig-zag course and the fact that the boat is climbing up and down waves. These latter errors are usually greatest with towed logs.

Tidal Streams

These were discussed in detail in chapter 4, and it should be apparent that they will have major effects on your dead reckoning plot.

Variation

This is the angular difference between True North, as marked on the chart, and Magnetic North, which is where your compass points. It changes from place to place, and also over periods of time. The amount, and the rate of change, will be noted on the compass roses on the chart.

Many charts have subsidiary Magnetic roses set inside the True roses, and if variation has changed negligibly since the chart was printed, you can simply work directly from the Magnetic rose and avoid the whole business of converting Magnetic courses and bearings to True for plotting.

Deviation

This is a measure of the magnetic influence your boat has on its steering compass. Metal in the boat, such as nails and

DEVIATION CARD Steering compass

Yacht **PAM**

Date **5th August 1987**

Magnetic course	Deviation	Compass course
000	2W	002
015	2W	017
030	3W	033
045	3W	048
060	4W	064
075	3W	078
090	3W	093
105	3W	108
120	2W	122
135	1W	136
150	1W	151
165	1W	166
180	0	180
195	0	195
210	0	210
225	0	225
240	1E	239
255	2E	253
270	2E	268
285	3E	282
300	2E	298
315	1E	314
330	0	330
345	1W	346
360	2W	002

Fig 23

engines, and magnetic fields embedded in it during construction (especially steel vessels) will pull the compass needle away from Magnetic North, creating an inbuilt error in all courses and bearings. This error varies with the heading of the boat. It can be reduced to a minimum by getting a qualified Compass Adjuster to 'swing the compass' onto a number of headings throughout the 360° and fix small magnets around the compass to compensate. The remaining small errors will be tabulated on a deviation card (see figure 23) and must be applied to all courses and bearings read off the main compass, in order to get an accurate figure that can be plotted on the Magnetic rose.

The main steering compass should be professionally swung at least every two years; every year if it is removed from the boat, as all sorts of errors can creep in during removal and storage. It should also be swung whenever any major work that might conceivably affect her residual magnetism is carried out on the boat – mainly changes in the engine or metal structure. If, having done this, you religiously ensure that nothing metallic or electrical (including small batteries) is moved within about three feet – less than a metre – of the compass (check the crew's pockets for torches, transistor radios and so on before they go on watch) then extraneous compass errors not recorded on the deviation card should not arise. Take every opportunity to

Photo 10 In a small boat it is not always easy to run an accurate DR plot because of difficult working conditions. It helps a lot if you keep plotting and calculating as simple as possible.

check the compass against the deviation card on a variety of headings using the methods described in chapter 6.

Adjusting the DR for Errors

It should be apparent from the foregoing that some experienced interpretation is necessary in order to assess the effects of all these influences. In my experience one of the secrets is to try *not* to be too accurate. There are sound reasons for this; the first being that figures that look accurate – 003½°; 16¾ nm; 22½ minutes and suchlike – tend to delude the navigator into thinking that they are accurate. Clearly, from the discussion so far, this kind of accuracy is quite unattainable when assessing (I deliberately refrain from the word 'calculate') such effects as leeway and helmsman's error. The second reason for not attempting such accuracy is that in practice a sequence of approximations tends to cancel out errors, leaving one

with a nice round figure of acceptable accuracy that creates no delusions about its precision. These round figures will also be found far easier to plot and calculate, and thus be less prone to error on a wild, dark night when the navigator is dog-tired and seasick. You may also find it instructive to measure the width of a blunt 2B pencil line on a small scale chart.

Knowing that his figures are approximate, the prudent navigator will then build sensible safety margins into his plot to allow for passing close to dangers.

Running the DR Plot

Figure 24 shows a basic DR plot, consisting of the course we wish to make good to our destination or a turning point ('course made good' – CMG), marked hourly at the distances we expect to travel; all plotted with no allowances made for any errors at all. These marked positions are known as 'dead reckoning'

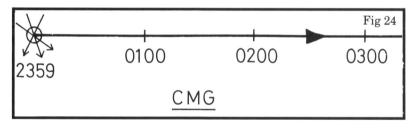

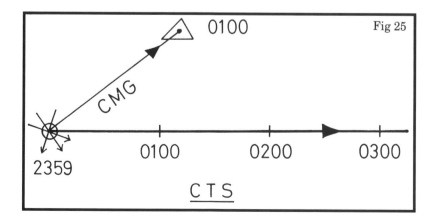

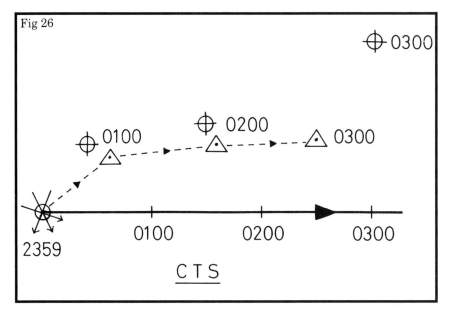

Fig 26

⊕ 0300

⊕ 0100   ⊕ 0200   △ 0300

△   △

0100   0200   0300

2359

C T S

positions (DR). Depending on the cir-cumstances, we can now either assess the errors beforehand and calculate a 'course to steer' (CTS) that will enable us to move along this track, or we can steer the plotted course, assessing the errors each hour in order to plot our actual 'es-timated position' (EP) as shown by the small triangle with its time in figure 25.

While proceeding along the passage this DR plot can (and should) be checked with fixes at every opportunity – be they traditional or electronic. With Decca or Satnav they can simply be read off the black box and marked on the chart at hourly intervals. A double cross-check then exists, in that the fixes enable the accuracy of error assessments to be tightened up, and the DR provides a check against wildly inaccurate fixes. If a fix is a long way out from the EP for the same time, then something clearly is wrong; there is an old saying that a DR track may not be very accurate but it is unlikely to be far out, whereas a duff fix could put you in the wrong ocean.

In figure 26 you can see a series of hourly DR positions together with EPs

calculated for the same times, and Decca fixes taken at those times. The gradual drift of the EPs away from the DRs has a definite look of normality about it, as do the first two Decca fixes. It should be apparent, however, that the Decca fix for 0300 is not right, and needs check-ing. It may be due simply to a mistake in reading or plotting, but the fact is it is an error that may not have been obvious to you without the DR plot for comparison.

Correcting for Compass Errors

Let us imagine we are steering a course A–B as in figure 27. The ship's compass reads 090°, which we call the compass course or CTS(C), being 'course to steer (compass)'. By applying the various compass errors according to the mnemonic CADET ('compass add east True'), it is simple to work out the Magnetic course being steered or the True course, either of which can then be plotted on the chart. On a recent chart with up-to-date variation it is simpler to work in Magnetic courses directly off the Magnetic rose. If the variation is outdated, then it is as well to convert to True. Contrary to popular opinion the mnemonic CADET covers all types of course conversion, and there is no need to remember anything about 'virgins being dull company' or whatever.

The sequence of corrections starts at Compass and ends at True, so those corrections closest to the compass come first; ie deviation then variation in that order, and the calculation can be halted at any stage. As we are proceeding here from Compass in the direction of True, add easterly errors and subtract westerly ones. Thus first apply to the CTS(C) deviation on that heading (from the deviation card); followed by variation if a True course is required. The end result is then the CTS(M) or CTS(T) as the case may be, as shown in figure 28. Although CTS is a traditional notation, this course would more properly be described as the 'course steered'.

Correcting for Sailing Errors

The chances of our small sailing boat actually moving along this line are, as already noted, extremely remote. The errors discussed above must now be

applied, in two stages. First apply leeway and helmsman's error so as to find the actual 'course through the water' (CTW); then apply the movement of the water itself (tidal stream etc) in order to arrive at the 'course made good' (CMG) over the ground. For convenience let us call the first lot 'drift', and the second lot 'set'. The application of drift to the CTS in order to find the CTW requires no mnemonic as the errors are directly relative to the compass course. It

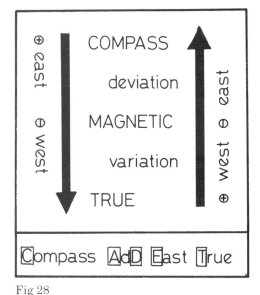

Fig 28

Fig 27

should be immediately apparent which way both leeway and helmsman's error must be applied. The resulting CTW can then be drawn on the chart, and it is to this actual course through the water that the combined set of tidal stream and current must be applied.

Correcting for Tidal Stream

Before we do this, let us make clear the distinction between tidal stream and current. The former is a variable flow of water caused by the changing tidal height, while the latter is a fixed flow of water caused by a variety of factors, such as salinity changes, and so on. It will be marked on charts and mentioned in Pilot Books. In addition, a movement of water known as 'surface drift' can be built up during long periods of strong steady winds, and a current of up to one knot (in the direction of the wind) can be experienced after two or three days of gales. Corrections for these currents (if they are experienced) are applied in exactly the same way as those for tidal stream.

Figure 29 shows how to apply these stream corrections. The line A–B represents the 'course through the water' (CTW). The distance AB is the distance moved through the water when we

decide to find out where the stream has set us to. If the course we will make good needs checking before we actually proceed along that line, then mark off any convenient distance (one hour's travel simplifies calculations – partly because tidal stream changes are recorded hourly, and partly because speeds of both stream and boat are measured in nautical miles per hour). This distance is taken either from an estimate of anticipated speed or from the log, as the case may be; the latter being corrected for any log error before plotting.

The direction and distance that the tidal stream will set us during this time is then found either from tidal diamonds on the chart or from the Tidal Stream Atlas and simply plotted from point B. Three arrows on the line indicate that it represents current or tidal stream. Point C is then the actual position (the EP) and the line A–C the course made good (CMG) over the ground. The distance AC represents the speed made good (SMG) over the ground, and is easily calculated if the distance AB has been taken for one hour or multiples thereof. Any other current or surface drift is then applied in identical fashion to point C until all movements of water during that time have been corrected for and a final position arrived at.

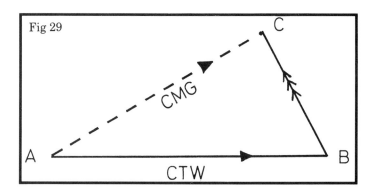

Fig 29

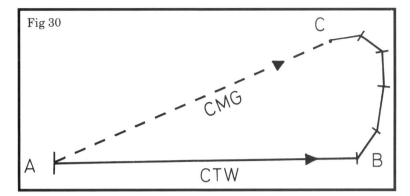

Fig 30

Correcting for Errors on Long Passages

On a passage longer than one hour, of course, the tidal stream changes constantly. If there are dangers close to either side of the course then a series of calculations like this must be made, one each hour or more frequently, depending on how far we can afford safely to drift off the course steered. Each new calculation must begin at point C, this being the actual place where the boat is (EP). A close check is thus kept on the boat's position as she moves with the stream. If, however, we are sailing in open waters and can safely drift about without danger of grounding etc, the whole series of calculations can be made in one fell swoop. The line A–B can be drawn all the way from departure point to destination, and the total passage time estimated according to predicted weather and so on. A series of tidal vectors for each hour of the passage can then be plotted in sequence from point B to indicate finally at point C where we will end up. This should be clear from figure 30. The total set during the passage from any fixed current must then be added to the plot before marking point C and plotting CMG and calculating SMG. Bear in mind that, as the passage progresses across the Tidal Stream Atlas, so the stream to be applied will change. A rough EP needs to be plotted hourly in order to check which stream arrow is affecting you at that time.

Allowing for Errors

Although it is essential to be able to correct for errors and find our true position on the chart, it is far more useful to calculate the errors beforehand and thus plot a course to steer that will actually take us to our destination, making allowance for the errors affecting us. The principle of this technique is very similar to the previous one except that all the errors are applied at the beginning of the CMG rather than at the end, and the order of their application is reversed. Thus calculate first the course we must travel through the water (CTW) so as to make allowance for stream and current; after which apply total drift, then the correct sequence of compass corrections, to finally arrive at the course to be steered according to the compass on the boat (CTS[C]). This is simpler and more logical than it sounds.

Allowing for Tidal Stream

In figure 31 you can see how it works. This time, the line A–B is the course we wish to make good (CMG). As before, take a one hour period and plot from A to

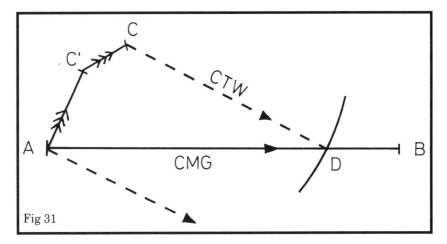

Fig 31

C the distance and direction the stream will take us in this time, plus (if necessary) any current. Although everything actually happens at the same time, this is clearer and easier to understand if we visualise them taking place separately. First the stream takes us from departure point A to point C′ in one hour. It then stops, and the current takes us in one hour from point C′ to point C. From point C we then have one hour in which to sail back onto the CMG. The result, as all these things actually happen at the same time, is that we move sideways along the line A–B, which is just what we want. Thus all we need do is take a pair of compasses set to the distance we estimate we will travel through the water in that hour, centre them on point C and mark where it intersects the line

A–B, at D. The line C–D (the CTW) is then the course we must sail at speed CD in order to move along the line A–B (the CMG) at speed AD. By plotting it from point A you can see clearly that as we sail off down the page, the stream and current will push us up until after one hour we are at point D.

Allowing for Sailing and Compass Errors

This, remember, is the course we must travel along through the water (CTW), and is unlikely to be the same as the course we need to steer on the compass. Leeway and helmsman's error must be allowed for to give a CTS(M) or CTS(T), depending on whether you are plotting in Magnetic or True. Variation and

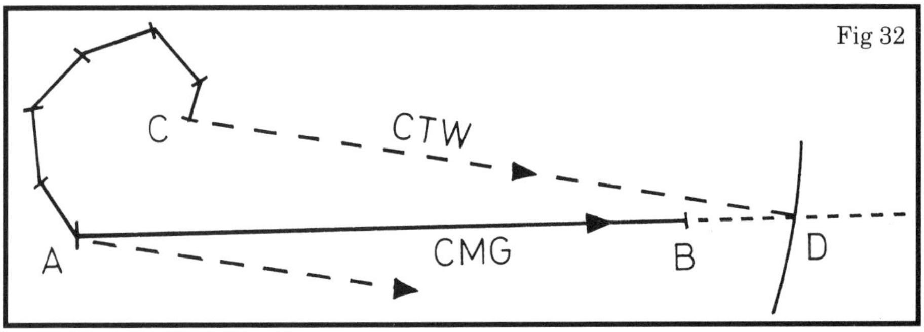

Fig 32

deviation must then be applied as required, using the mnemonic CADET, but in reverse, as we are now moving towards the Compass from True or Magnetic (as the case may be). This time westerly errors are added and easterly ones subtracted. Variation is applied first if the plotting is in True; then deviation for that course (heading). The result is the compass course to steer – CTS(C) (see figure 28).

Allowing for Errors on Long Passages

The same basic technique can be used for a long passage spanning a number of changing tidal streams. Total them up by plotting them one after the other from point A, as described above in the section on 'correcting for errors'. It should be apparent from figure 32, however, that if the overall tidal set is any more than minimal it will produce a passage time rather different from the one used to calculate the total set; SMG (with tidal influence) being AD, which is faster than AB (used to assess the total set). In this example we will pass our destination before experiencing all the tidal vectors used in plotting the CTW, so the CTW will be wrong. If this difference (BD) is small we can simply ignore it, on the assumption that our estimated average speed for a long passage under sail will be only approximate anyway. Thus all we need do is to reassess the average speed when somewhere near our destination, plot an EP as described above, then recalculate the CTW from here using the new estimated speed and the tidal vectors during this final leg of the passage. The inherent error in this last calculation will be very small, due to the short distance involved.

If the overall set produces a passage time that is wildly different from the one used for assessing the set, then a further, more accurate plot of the CTW can be made by using the new passage time to replot the overall set. This will give a much smaller error, in the opposite direction, and the process can be repeated if necessary until points B and D are close enough for the accuracy desired. If this sounds confusing, then visualise C–D replotted with fewer tidal vectors and it should become clear. The CTW can then be converted into a CTS(C) for us to steer (see figure 28).

Checking Track for Dangers

It is most important when plotting a course in this manner, to check carefully along either side of the CMG on the chart to ensure that you will not be set into danger as the boat drifts possibly quite a long way to the side during the passage. If dangers exist close on either side of the CMG then a series of CTWs must be calculated each hour, so as to keep the boat close to the CMG. This may be advisable also in certain changing wind conditions, and this question will be discussed in chapter 13.

Course Notations

The notation I have used for courses is based on the system I learnt in the Navy and I find it logical, memorable and convenient. It is also quick to write in notebooks and logbooks, especially when suffixed with (C), (M), or (T) for precision. For the RYA system, use ground track for CMG, water track for CTW and heading for CTS.

6
Coastal Fixing

The DR plot should be checked whenever possible by fixing the position of the boat, bearing in mind what was said in chapter 5 about this being a two-way check: the DR checking the fix, as well as the fix checking the DR. The principle of all coastal fixing is based on the crossing of two or more position lines; if we know that we are on both lines somewhere, then clearly the point at which they cross is precisely where we are. The precision, or accuracy, of the fix is dependent on the accuracy of both position lines, and this can be determined by the simple expedient of using a third position line. If all three cross exactly together then (with certain exceptions to be considered later) we can say that the fix accurately represents our precise position at the time of measuring the position lines. If they do not cross together – forming a triangle called a 'cocked hat' – then this indicates inaccuracy somewhere – probably caused by incorrect identification, measurement or plotting of one or more of the position lines, or by an error in the compass used to take the bearings.

Position Lines

These position lines can come from a variety of sources: compass bearings of prominent fixed objects (lighthouses, trees, buildings etc); transits (bearings of two prominent objects in line); depth contours; horizontal and vertical sextant angles; radar ranges and bearings; RDF bearings; astronomical observations; lighthouse dipping ranges, and so on. Any of these may be used in a variety of combinations to produce a fix, although some are more accurate than others. If a cocked hat is obtained, it should be possible to ascertain with reasonable accuracy which part of it the boat is in, by weighing up all the known inaccuracies. If, for example, the EP is close to the two most accurate position lines then this corner of the cocked hat is probably the position of the boat. If in any doubt, the boat should be assumed to be at the corner nearest to danger.

Accuracy of Position Lines

Take the variety of position lines that we can use for fixing and consider their relative accuracies and the ease with which they can be obtained. It is important to appreciate that a position line that is both quick and simple to take and plot may in practice prove more accurate and reliable in pilotage conditions than one that is theoretically better but more difficult to obtain.

Visual Compass Bearing: the classic position line – simple to take, easy to plot, and accurate (subject to the provisos in the next section).

Transit: the most accurate of all position lines as it is not dependent on magnetic influences, weather conditions and suchlike; but rarely available when required. Best use is as a clearing line and as such will be discussed in chapter 8.

Horizontal Sextant Angle: extremely accurate but requires skill to take and knowledge of geometry or the use of special instruments to plot. I have used it in survey work in the Navy, but never during normal sailing.

Angular Difference: a similar position line can be achieved, less accurately, using the angular difference between two compass bearings. A carefully shot two point fix is probably more useful in practice to a small boat navigator (although an angular difference eliminates any compass error); the plotting is shown in figure 33 in case you are interested.

Range by Horizontal Angle: a good range can be calculated by measuring the horizontal angle between two close

Fig 33 *The measured angular difference between two objects (whether from compass bearings or horizontal sextant angle) places the boat on a position line consisting of the circle shown. As the angle subtended by a chord at the centre of a circle is twice that subtended at the circumference, the centre of this circle (O) can be plotted as shown, and a curved position line drawn. With three objects, two circles are obtained, producing a fix from two crossed position lines.*

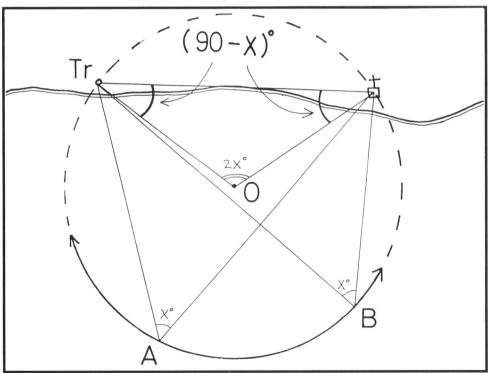

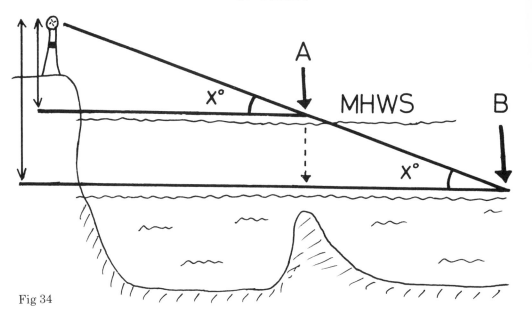

Fig 34

objects that are roughly on the beam (less than 25° apart), using either sextant (most accurate) or compass bearings. The right and left hand edges of a small island would be a good example. A scientific calculator is useful as the formula is – Range = (½ × distance apart of objects) × Cotangent (½ × angular difference). A more approximate version is – Range = (57 × distance apart) ÷ angular difference.

Vertical Sextant Angle: if you have a sextant, this is easier to take and plot, and more useful than the horizontal variety. It will give an accurate distance off a lighthouse etc, and can be combined with a compass bearing of the same object to give a rare example of a good two point fix. Nautical Almanacs contain tables that can be entered with the height of the object and its angle above sea level, to give a distance off.

It is important to understand precisely what is meant by the noted height of a lighthouse. The height given on a chart is the height of the light itself (not

the building) above MHWS (mean high water springs). Thus the angle should be measured to the centre of the light, not to the top of the lighthouse. A correction should also be made to the measured height to allow for the actual sea level at the time, caused by the height of tide. If the height of the tide at the time of taking the angle is lower than MHWS then the actual height of the light will be increased by the difference in the tidal heights (see figure 34). Make sure also that the height is being measured from the base of the light or cliff at sea level and that this base is not in fact below the horizon.

Many authorities claim that this difference can be ignored, as the height of tide is likely to be less than MHWS thus causing the light to appear higher, and therefore closer than it actually is. This is claimed to create an automatic safety factor. If, however, you are checking your distance off in order to ensure passing inside an off-lying danger (see chapter 8), or if you are on top of a big spring tide that is higher than MHWS, then it could get you into a great deal of trouble. The effort involved in mentally calculating the difference between the tidal height and MHWS, then applying this to the charted height of a light seems insufficiently arduous to justify building an unnecessary error into your distance off.

Dipping Range: this is a useful, although approximate, modification of the above, particularly helpful when making landfall at night. The moment a light appears over the horizon is dependent on its height and the height of your eye, and these can be entered in tables in the Almanac to give a range of the light (see figure 35). Crossed with a bearing of the light this can give a useful initial landfall fix.

RDF Bearing: this is fraught with all sorts of potential inaccuracies and needs to be used with some care and experience, although plotting is as easy as with visual bearings (see chapter 14 for details).

Radar Bearing: easy to take and plot, but often difficult to identify with certainty precisely where on the chart the bearing is taken from. Inherently inaccurate due to the width of the radar beam and the fact that the bearing is relative to the ship's head which is possibly yawing (see chapter 10).

Radar Range: same comments about identification apply, although inherent accuracy is much greater than that with a bearing.

Depth Sounding: easy to take, but vague and inaccurate to plot unless bottom slopes steeply and regularly with clearly marked contours. It can, however, be a useful check on the general whereabouts of a fix taken by other means. Remember to reduce to soundings before plotting, so as to allow for tidal height (see chapter 4).

Accuracy in Fixing

Whatever is used for obtaining a position line, we can take various measures to ensure maximum accuracy:

1 – use handbearing and RDF compasses in a place on the boat known to be free of magnetic or metallic influences.

2 – use three position lines that cross at as near to 60° as possible (or two crossing at 90°). With shallow cuts, slight errors are magnified considerably (see figure 36).

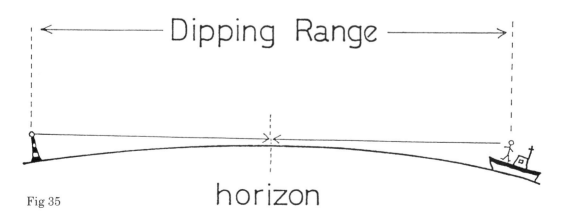

Fig 35

← Dipping Range →

horizon

3 – visual bearings of near objects are more accurate than those of distant objects, as slight errors will increase with the length of the plotted bearing (see figure 37).

Selection of Objects

Use objects that are static, reliably identified and clearly defined. Man-made transits, lighthouses, objects marked (conspic), straight depth contours on a steeply shelving bottom, high vertical headlands and suchlike all fit this category. Buoys can drag out of position (less likely close to large commercial harbours); radar ranges can easily be taken of wrong objects (especially high ground and headlands) as the echo may not be returning from precisely where you think; depth contours on shallow slopes are extremely inaccurate and unreliable for fairly obvious reasons; certain shelving headlands can vary their positions according to the height of tide if the range is large (see figure 38).

Photo 11 *Buoys are not reliable objects for fixing on, although those in rivers and close to harbours (like this one) are much better than ones in exposed offshore positions. The tower on the left, however, is an excellent fixing feature, being clearly and easily recognisable from a considerable distance.*

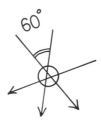

Fig 36

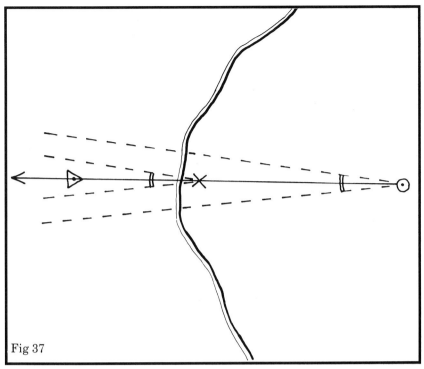

Fig 37

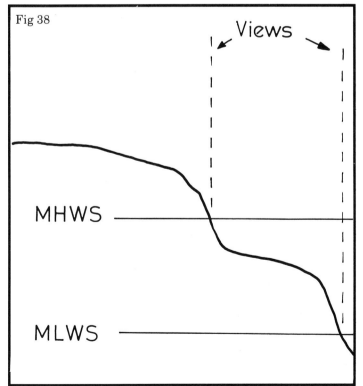

Fig 38

Views

MHWS

MLWS

Remember that objects that look clear and obvious when viewed vertically on a chart may not be so when viewed horizontally from the boat. Jetties and headlands are classic examples. Even objects marked (conspic) must be treated with caution as often similar things close by are more conspicuous although not marked as such. Conspicuous trees may be cut down at short notice, leaving another conspicuous one half a mile to one side. Trees may also grow up and new buildings may obscure objects (conspic), so identification of such things must be made with some care (see chapters 2 and 3).

The Circular Fix

If compass bearings are taken of three objects that happen to lie on the circumference of a circle passing through the boat's position, then a perfect-looking fix can ensue, even with a huge compass error. For geometrical reasons the three bearings will always cross at a point, with no cocked hat to indicate an error. Although the odds of this happening may be fairly small, it is worth being wary of any three point fix taken when the centre object is further away

Fig 39 *A careful study of figure 33 will show why this problem arises. In principle the three objects here are joined by two chords of the same position circle with the result that two angular differences are generated, each producing this same circle as a position line. In effect it could be likened to shooting a three-point fix when all the objects are in line, so that the three position lines lie on top of one another.*

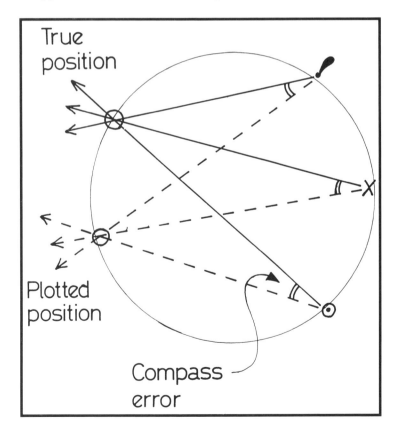

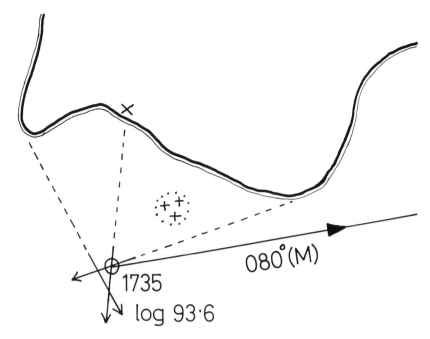

080°(M)

1735

log 93·6

Fig 40

than the outer ones. You can see what happens in figure 39. The solid lines show the actual bearings and where they meet, while the pecked ones show bearings plotted from a compass with an error.

Taking and Plotting the Fix

Bearing in mind all the points made above, the first thing is to select the position lines you intend to use. There is no reason why you should not use more than three if more are available, but you must consider any inaccuracy that may be caused by the time needed to take them all. If the Magnetic compass rose on the chart is out of date, then all compass bearings should be converted to True and plotted as such, applying variation according to the mnemonic CADET as explained in chapter 5.

Take the sequence of bearings as rapidly as possible, especially when sailing fast, or the boat will be in a different place for each position line. The result will be a large cocked hat. Take bearings ahead or astern first (as these will be changing least rapidly), then time the fix for the final bearing on the beam, as the value of this will be changing the fastest. Make sure the compass card settles for each bearing.

There is no need to draw the bearing line all the way from the object to your rough position; it wears out both chart and pencil (and clutters up the plot unnecessarily). A one-inch line in the right place is quite sufficient. If a good cut, or at least a reasonable cocked hat, ensues, then you can circle the intersection that you decide is nearest to your position (see above) and mark it with both the time of taking and the log reading at that time (see figure 40). Brief details of the fix and its time should be entered in the logbook in case someone spills cocoa over the chart. Symbols such as |← or LHE (Lefthand edge of land), (c) for (conspic), + for church, and

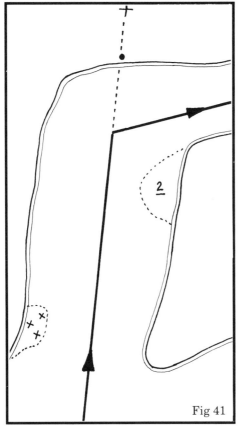

Fig 41

spaced 60° apart just are not available. A common situation is when only one or two objects are available for fixing on. In the latter case a perfectly accurate fix may be obtained if the bearings cross at nearly 90° (as opposed to the 60° required for a good three-point fix), but there will be no means of checking its accuracy other than by comparison with an EP for the same time – no cocked hat to show up errors. All possible means should be employed in order to assess the accuracy of such a two-point fix – a sounding often being a useful guide even if circumstances do not make it good enough for an actual position line. With a single object we will not get a position at all – just a line on which we probably lie somewhere.

The Single Position Line

There are two ways of viewing a single position line: negatively, as being a pretty useless indication of where you are; or positively, as a very good indication of where you are not. This latter viewpoint is not as silly as it sounds. A transit is the most accurate position line you can get, and it should be apparent from figure 41 that although following the transit up the estuary does not tell you where you are, it does reliably inform you that you are not in the dangerous waters on either side of it. Progress in a situation such as this can be gauged quite accurately by crossing the transit with bearings of objects ashore, or in suitable circumstances by simply checking depths on the echo-sounder.

A particularly useful application of transits is not so much for getting a position line as for marking the boundary of dangerous waters – banks, rocks, etc. By keeping the boat to one side of the line you can be sure of avoiding the danger, even if you do not actually know

so on will keep it short and tidy. Mark the bearings either True or Magnetic ([T] or [M]) to avoid possible confusion later. An example might be: 0925 |← Berry Head 175°(M); +Tr Hollicombe Hd 320°(M); Ore Stone 040°(M); log 23.5; depth 12.5m. A sounding like this is often handy, not as part of the fix (unless conditions suit), but as a general check that no major error exists in either the compass or the brain. This particular fix is close to a small patch under ten metres, so if the sounding had indicated this shallow depth, it would have been a valuable guide to the accuracy of the fix.

Uncertain Fixes

Naturally there will be occasions on which three nice clear position lines

Photo 12 *The buoy in transit with the white house tucked in the trees will lead safely clear of any dangers either side of that track, but bear in mind what was said earlier about the reliability of a buoy's position. An off-lying beacon or second shore mark would be better.*

precisely where you are (see chapter 8).

At certain times soundings of depth contours can produce extremely useful position lines. A clearly defined contour parallel to a coastline can, for example, provide a very reasonable distance off when closing the land in fog, and this same contour can often then be followed round a headland into an estuary or bay where the anchor can be let go safely. It may even at times be possible to get a usable fix by following a depth contour until it turns sharply, to swing out of a narrow bay perhaps. Position fixing with an echo-sounder is clearly useful especially in poor visibility, and this aspect of it is dealt with in more detail in chapter 10.

The Transferred Position Line

This is a very convenient way to utilise a single position line, as long as the inherent inaccuracies are fully understood. If the first bearing can be run on to join a two-point fix, or a two-point fix run on to join a later bearing, the resulting cocked hat should give some indication of the accuracy. Some care will be needed in this situation to ensure that all three bearings lie about 60° apart, or even greater errors are likely to result.

The Running Fix

A common use of the transferred position line is the 'running fix', in which a second bearing is taken of the same

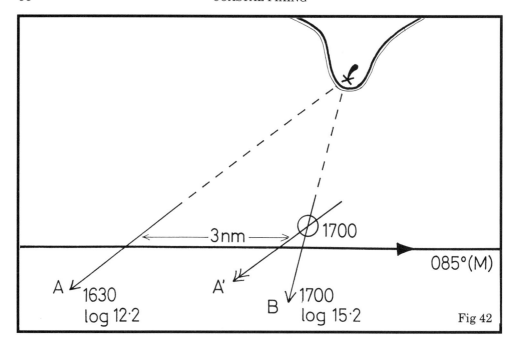

3nm

1700

085°(M)

A   1630
    log 12·2

A'

B   1700
    log 15·2

Fig 42

object some time later (ideally when the bearings have drawn about 90° apart) and the first bearing run on the distance and direction travelled between the bearings. This can be done equally well with bearings of two separate objects (if the first is lost in fog, for example). In figure 42, with no tidal stream or leeway, a bearing A is taken of the lighthouse at 1630 when the log reads 12.2. At 1700 a second bearing B is taken of the lighthouse and the log reading noted as 15.2. The first bearing is then moved 3 miles along the course and replotted as A' to give the two-point fix shown. In the simple conditions described – no stream or leeway, and a steady course steered – this will produce quite a reasonable position, although not as good as a three- point, or even a careful two-point fix.

The accuracy of a running fix rapidly diminishes, however, when tidal stream and leeway combine to add probable errors to the distance and direction that the first position line has to be run on. In

such conditions the course and distance made good over the ground between the bearings must be plotted as described in chapter 5, and the first bearing run on that distance in that direction (see figure 43).

Special Running Fixes

There are certain specialised types of running fix that are particularly useful when piloting, as they produce distances off without having to do any chart plotting or complicated calculations. They are, however, really practical only in conditions of no tidal stream or leeway (see chapter 8).

The Position Circle

When a fix has been obtained from position lines of dubious accuracy, all too many navigators mark a cross on the chart then say to themselves: 'That is where we are; I hope.' This is not

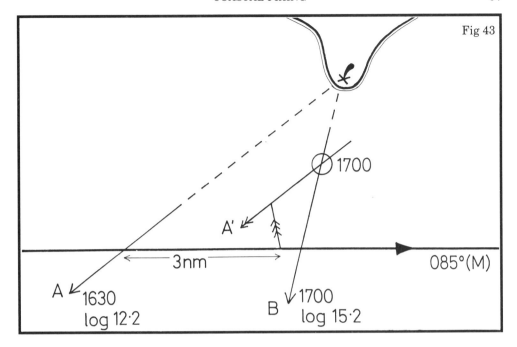

Fig 43

1700

A'

←——3nm——→   085°(M)

A 1630
   log 12·2

B 1700
   log 15·2

a very constructive way of navigating in such circumstances, if only because it creates mixed feelings of hope and worry in the skipper's mind. A more positive approach is to estimate the maximum possible errors for each position line and plot a box containing all the possible positions obtained from all the combinations of errors. You can then say with certainty that you are in that box somewhere. From then on, instead of manoeuvring a point around the chart in the hope that you are somewhere near it, you can manoeuvre the box around the chart, knowing that you are definitely in it, somewhere.

This technique is known as using a position circle, as in its simplest form it consists of drawing a circle around the fix with a radius of the maximum estimated distance you could be from it. Whether you use this simple circle or a more complex (and accurate) box matters not; the principle of moving it around the chart to keep it in safe water until a good fix can be obtained remains

the same. Very often this box can be reduced in size gradually by stages, using single position lines or soundings that are reasonably accurate, and all means of reducing its size should be sought constantly, rather than simply waiting for a good three-point fix to come along. A good example of this technique is described in chapter 10.

The essence of this system is its certainty; however large the box may be, the technique is as safe as houses so long as you are absolutely sure you are in the box. So never skimp on the estimate of errors; plot them as large as they could possibly be. It is more important in this type of navigation to know with certainty where you are not, than it is to know roughly where you are.

Shooting up a Feature

There may be occasions when you have two clearly identified features for compass bearings, together with a third whose identification is uncertain. There

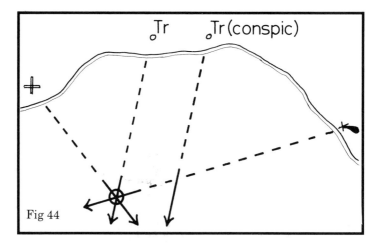

Fig 44

is a simple way to check the identity of the third feature and thus enable a proper three-point fix to be shot and it is referred to as 'shooting up'.

The fix should be shot in the normal way to get bearings of all three features. The two bearings from the known objects should then be plotted on the chart as a two-point fix. The third bearing is then plotted in reverse – ie from the two-point fix instead of from the suspect object. This line should then pass through the object that the original bearing was taken on (see figure 44). This is in a sense using the result to prove itself, and there will be no cocked hat to indicate errors, so it must be used with some caution. In most cases, however, you will probably find that it works in practice, as it should be quite clear whether you have the right object or whether doubt exists.

A variation of the method involves taking the bearing of an unidentified object in transit with a known one. By plotting the bearing through the known object it should indicate which feature on the chart is the one in transit. This is a useful trick for identifying buoys. The precise position of a buoy can even be ascertained by plotting a series of three

such transits. Details of the method are described in chapter 9, where it is used for plotting the position of another vessel in an anchorage you are approaching. Strictly speaking, this shooting up should be done before relying on a buoy for navigation.

Checking the Compass

This is a vitally important part of both fixing and of dead reckoning. Every opportunity should be taken to check both steering and hand-bearing compasses as frequently as possible, by whatever means is available.

The first part of this continuous process should be to ascertain where on deck you can stand with the hand-bearing compass and not have it affected by deviation. As soon as possible after the steering compass has been swung (so that you know the accuracy of that), you should wander about the deck taking readings from the hand-bearing compass and checking them against the deviation-corrected readings of the main compass. Do this on a variety of headings until you find a place where no deviation effects are registered on the hand-bearing compass. Note the precise position of this place in the back of the log, and ensure that all compass bearings are always taken from there. If you find a selection of places then pick one where you can operate in bad weather.

Thereafter, the steering compass can always be routinely checked against the heading shown on the hand-bearing compass. This will be most accurate if you find a deviation-free place on the centreline for using the hand-bearer.

Both compasses should, however, be checked against fixed lines of bearing ashore whenever possible. The best type of line for this is a transit as it is not influenced in any way by magnetism, tidal streams or anything else, and it produces a very clear, precise and accurate line to sight on. Charted transits always have their bearings marked alongside them, and these bearings are noted in degrees True as viewed from seaward. By applying the local variation to the bearing, as explained in chapter 5, you can convert it to Magnetic, and this should agree with the bearing obtained from the hand-bearing compass and also that from the steering compass corrected for deviation. The easiest way to do this check is simply to motor along the transit so that both compasses have plenty of time to settle down. You should try over a period of time to gain checks from transits running in a variety of directions, each transit being used also to check its reciprocal bearing, as deviation varies with the vessel's heading.

There are various other ways of checking compasses – taking the azimuth of the sun at sunrise for example – but transits provide by far the most accurate and useful in coastal sailing. Care must be taken, however, to check steering compasses in tideless conditions as the boat must be steered directly along the transit.

7

Inshore Dangers

By and large there are many more dangers to navigation close inshore than ever there are out at sea. The biggest one, of course, is the land itself; boats are much happier bouncing around in waves than they are bouncing around on beaches or on rocks or sandbanks. Most of the dangers that concern us are marked on charts, but many are not. Even those that are will not be clearly evident unless the navigational position of the vessel is precise. It is essential that the coastal pilot be able to both foresee and observe the existence of inshore dangers. Let us therefore consider these dangers in their loose categories as detailed below.

Depth of Water

Sandbanks, rocks, wrecks, river bars, and so on, can all cause serious local reductions in the depth of water you generally are sailing in. By and large all these hazards will be marked on charts, but it is important to know the precise meanings of the symbols in terms of the amount of water to be found over them. *Admiralty Chart Booklet 5011* gives full details of all symbols on Admiralty charts and should be studied with care if you use those charts. Other charts tend to be less cryptic and more informative,

and their symbols need to be checked closely.

Many of these objects, while dangerous at or near Low Water, will often be quite safe for a small boat to sail over after half-flood. If you have noted the height of tide for the area for each hour of the passage in your navigator's notebook (see chapter 2) it will be the work of a moment to calculate whether you can safely pass over them or not. You should always, however, leave a good safety margin to allow for meteorological or other factors affecting the true height of the tide (see chapter 4). You should also make allowance for any sea or swell that could drop you, in the troughs, much closer to the bottom than your tidal calculations say you are. Large submerged objects like sandbanks or river bars can cause otherwise innocuous seas to steepen and rise (see next two sections), thus producing correspondingly deep troughs into which you can fall and make a mockery of your tidal sums.

It can be instructive on a quiet afternoon at sea, or in front of the fire in wintertime, to measure the distance between the soundings on some of your charts. Unless they have been surveyed very recently with modern side-scan sonar there may be large areas between

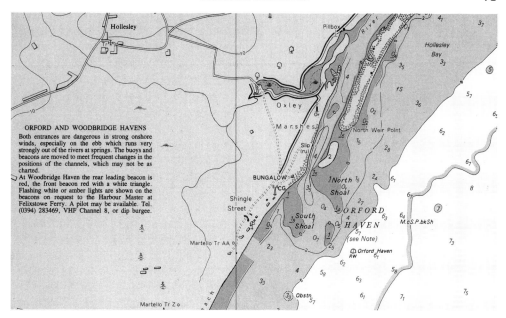

Fig 45 *See the comments under the heading ORFORD AND WOODBRIDGE HAVENS at top left.*

the lines of soundings that have never actually been sounded. In areas with an uneven seabed it is possible that a high lump has escaped the survey vessel and is lying in wait for you. There is probably little you can actually do about this, but it behoves the cautious pilot to give himself a good safety margin of depth at all times, and particularly if he is in sparsely sounded areas and using an old chart. If you do find a shallow patch that is not marked on your chart the Hydrographer of the Navy will doubtless be pleased to hear from you!

Sandbanks

In areas where sandbanks are found it is not uncommon for these to shift about rather a lot, especially after onshore gales, and it is vital that large-scale, up-to-date charts are used when navigating such places (see figure 45).

The local Pilot Book should also be studied carefully along with the most recent supplements. If in any doubt then allow very large margins of error in such waters and always try to negotiate them on a rising tide while it is still low enough to show the banks. An echo-sounder or leadline may not give sufficient warning of a steep-to bank for the boat to alter course away from it. Sand may not be as hard as rock but it can do a great deal of damage to a boat that is pounding on it in any kind of swell. Often there can be useful indications of where banks lie, according to the sea state, and details will be found in chapter 11.

Be on the lookout also for buoys that appear to be out of position according to your chart in places like this. They may have been moved recently to accommodate a change in the channel. The Pilot Book will probably advise on the likelihood of this. Be aware, however, of the possibility that the buoy may simply have dragged out of position.

Sandbanks do have their good points

in that they can provide very useful shelter at times in otherwise open waters. Even in a hard onshore blow, the lee side of an exposed bank will have relatively smooth water, and in areas where long lengths of overlapping banks run along the coast it is often possible to make passages in quite calm water when conditions outside the banks are ferocious. But make very careful note of the tidal heights, or you could find yourself suddenly exposed to the full blast of the sea as the tide rises over the banks. Even part-submerged banks can give surprisingly good shelter because the very shallow water over them breaks the seas and robs them of their energy, leaving much quieter waters to leeward.

River Bars

These are rather specialised sandbanks that often pile up in the mouths of rivers, creating very shallow humps right across the entrances. Best water is indicated generally by some sort of transit or leading marks (see chapter 8). Many river bars change shape, depth and position frequently, and the leading marks will be shifted periodically to accommodate this. Pilot Books will advise, but it is essential to realise that there may be delays between the bar changing and the marks being shifted, so large safety margins must always be allowed when crossing such bars.

It is generally most unwise to follow another vessel over a shifting bar, except by prior arrangement. Not only may he draw less than you, but if he is local he may follow a tortuous route that you will be unable to stick to. Often the deepest water may be identified, especially in choppy weather, by observing the appearance of the water (see chapters 8 and 11).

Very dangerous breaking seas frequently occur on bars in strong onshore winds, especially on the ebb (see next section). These waves are difficult to spot when approaching from seaward, as they are so localised, and bars should be treated with utmost caution in conditions that may cause them. Generally the safest time to cross is near the top of the flood tide, when there is maximum depth of water and the stream is running with the wind.

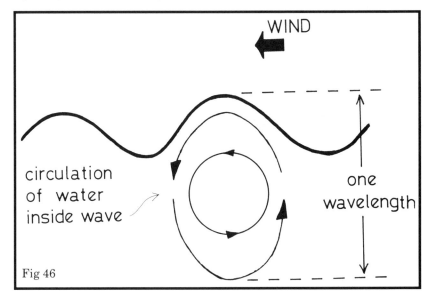

WIND

circulation of water inside wave

one wavelength

Fig 46

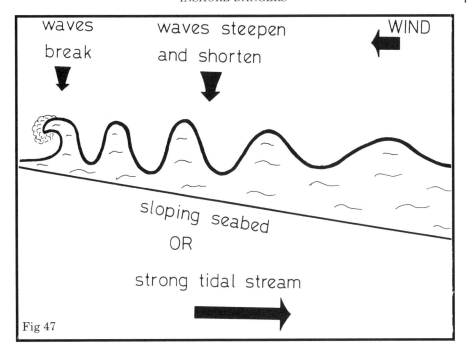

waves break

waves steepen and shorten

WIND

sloping seabed

OR

strong tidal stream

Fig 47

Behaviour of Waves

The basic problem here is the effects of shallow water, strong tides, jetties, cliffs, headlands, etc, on the otherwise smooth and harmless passage of the waves. In principle we can say that shallow water or strong tides will slow down the lower parts of waves, thus forcing their energy upwards to create seas steeper, shorter and higher than normal. Waves are not lumps of water moving along the sea but energy exciting the water. This energy causes water to flow round in each wave that it generates, and the depth the water circulation reaches is roughly equal to the length of the wave (see figure 46). Shallow water (close to the wavelength in depth) or strong, opposing, tidal streams will slow down the lower part of this circulation, forcing the energy upwards into the top half of the wave. This causes following waves to bunch up as the first ones slow down, resulting in the waves growing steeper, higher and shorter in

wavelength. If the process goes on long enough the waves become top-heavy and break – solid water cascading down the front of them (see figure 47).

Reflection and Refraction

Waves are also affected by solid objects such as cliffs and jetties, being refracted and reflected according to the angle at which they strike (see figure 48). The waves then run back into those following them, thus causing steep, short and confused seas that can be dangerous to small boats.

Shoal Water

The main danger to a small boat comes from the steepness of the waves making steering difficult, and forward movement very slow if she is heading into them, due to the poor boat 'bouncing up and down in the same hole' as each steep wave stops her dead. Beating off a lee shore in such seas could

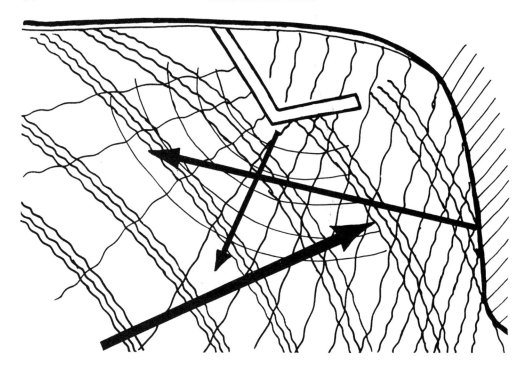

Fig 48 *The main wavetrain comes from seaward as indicated by the broad arrow at bottom left. These waves are reflected both from the cliffs to the right and from the harbour breakwater, as shown by the other two arrows. Refraction will also occur at the breakwater, and the resulting waves running in all directions will create a very rough and confused sea in the approaches to the harbour entrance.*

verge on the impossible for a small sailing vessel. Then there is the potential damage from huge weights of solid water crashing onto hatches, windows, etc, creating serious risk of flooding or even of foundering. A small dinghy full of sea water weighs about a ton.

All this can be seen any day on any beach with a strong onshore wind blowing, and it takes little imagination to visualise what can happen to a small boat caught in such waves. Go offshore half a mile or so and you could probably happily row round in a dinghy. However, the fact that strong tidal streams running against the wind create similar effects is not always appreciated.

Wind against Tide

In many places the difference between conditions during a lee-going and a weather-going stream is simply one of some discomfort, but where streams run hard – say three knots or more – the difference can be quite alarming. A sea that rolls along peaceably all morning with the flood stream under it can turn into a maelstrom when the tide turns and a big spring ebb runs hard into it. Careful judging of the tidal streams can make a considerable difference to the comfort and safety of many a coastal passage in rough weather.

Rips, Races and Overfalls

When seas or tidal streams run in from differing directions and meet at all angles the effects are even worse. Particularly bad seas tend to be caused off headlands, where tidal streams converge from different directions then swirl about (see chapter 4). The Race off Portland Bill in the English Channel is a well-known example, and there are many such places in and around the Pentland Firth, north of Scotland, where very fast tides run through a relatively narrow channel into which several headlands protrude. If the seabed is uneven, very strong tides can create swirls and eddies, which can often cause extremely broken, irregular seas and even whirlpools, as in the Gulf of Corryvreckan on the Scottish West Coast. Similar conditions can be generated by underwater obstacles, such as banks and rocky ledges, causing strong tidal streams to divert and meet again at different angles.

The danger in all these situations is that steep, breaking seas from a multitude of directions will throw a small boat around horribly, and may even swamp her through the sheer weight of water crashing onboard. The interaction of many different trains of waves can cause very deep troughs and very high waves when different ones coincide, and this can be an even greater danger. The very strong, swirling tidal streams can also carry a low-powered vessel quite out of control onto the rocks. Such areas should be avoided in any strength

Photo 13 Tidal eddies and rips in the Scottish Western Isles, caused by strong tidal streams meeting and running over uneven seabeds. In strong winds such places could be extremely dangerous for small boats.

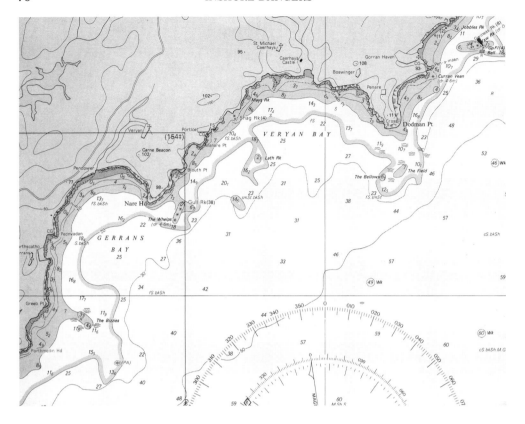

Fig 49 *Overfalls can be seen close south of Dodman Point and also over The Bizzies, south of Gerrans Bay. The former will be caused largely by the tidal streams rounding the headland, and the latter by the shallow patches and uneven bottom.*

of wind and stream, and they will be clearly marked on the chart as overfalls, races, tide-rips or eddies (see figure 49). Local Pilot Books will give more detail.

Coastal Winds

A number of particular wind effects can cause concern to the inshore pilot. The obvious one, of course, is the simple matter of a lee shore. Dismasting or an engine breakdown on a lee shore in any kind of weather is very serious, as it is not usually feasible to anchor in

such conditions. The closer to the shore the vessel drifts, the worse the seas will become (see previous section), so it is sound pilotage to hold as far off a lee shore as possible while coasting, so that if trouble does arise there will be both reasonably smooth seas and time in which to sort it out.

The Sea Breeze

The sea breeze is a well-known phenomenon that is welcomed by sailors in the calm anticyclonic conditions in which it normally occurs. This wind is caused by the land heating up in hot weather faster than the sea. The warm air over the land rises and draws cooler air off the sea to replace it. An onshore wind, known as the sea breeze, is thus generated, extending perhaps ten or twenty miles offshore (see figure 50). It generally begins around mid- to late-morning when the land has had time to heat up, and it dies away early in the evening as the land cools again. During the day the rotation of the Earth causes this wind to veer steadily in the Northern Hemisphere, due to the Coriolis Force. The sea breeze is most marked in late spring and summer when the sea is still cool from the winter and the sun is hot.

It should be borne in mind that in certain circumstances this pleasant little sailing sea breeze (rarely more than force 3/4) can grow to virtually an onshore gale. By and large, the hotter the weather the stronger the sea breeze. If a wind is already blowing onshore, very hot weather could cause a strong enough sea breeze to reinforce this existing wind to almost gale force. If a south-facing coastline slopes up gently, the heating of the land is greater than when the land is flat, and further wind is generated to reinforce the sea breeze.

This is known as an anabatic wind. A sailor in trouble in this onshore wind knows that he has only to keep off the shore until the evening, or beat out ten miles or so, when it will all die down again.

The Land Breeze

In very hot weather, generally in Mediterranean or tropical areas, the land continues cooling during the evening to below the temperature of the sea, whereupon warmer air over the sea begins rising and a land breeze (offshore) is set up during the night. Very occasionally this may be noticed in temperate climates in exceptionally hot weather, particularly up river estuaries where shallow water has been warmed during the day to higher than the sea temperature. Autumn is the most likely time, when the sea is warmest. The land breeze rarely reaches more than a few miles offshore except on extremely

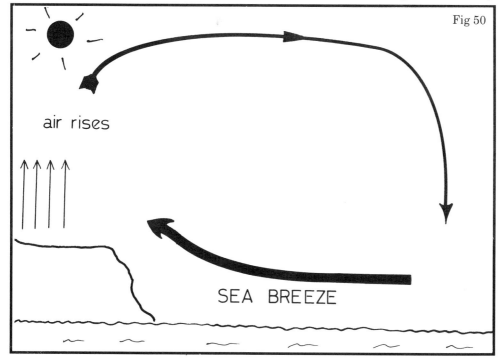

Fig 50

air rises

SEA BREEZE

hot desert coasts, which cool very rapidly at night.

Katabatic Winds

In certain places, especially when under sail, even an offshore breeze can cause problems. Where high, steep mountains border the shoreline – such as in Scottish lochs, Norwegian fjords, etc – the air cools during the evening at the tops of the mountains, then falls down the slopes and funnels through the valleys, and can generate very strong nocturnal winds called katabatic winds. These can make both anchoring and sailing in such places a rather uncomfortable business, as these winds tend to be rather sudden and squally, and can descend almost vertically onto an unsuspecting boat. If the katabatic wind is reinforced by a land breeze it will be even stronger.

In areas where particularly high, cold, mountains border the coast, this katabatic wind can occur during the daytime, the very cold wind falling down the mountainside regardless of the weather effects.

Geographical Influences

The presence of the land can cause winds to bend and accelerate at times, much like tidal streams do (see chapter 4). Like a stream, the wind will tend to take the easiest route past obstacles, which is often round rather than over the top. High headlands can divert a wind blowing along the shore out to sea or inland, and this wind will be accelerated as it rushes round the longer distance. In some places very strong winds like this can even cause back eddies to leeward of the headland, much as a tidal stream does.

Even a wind blowing at a slight angle onto a high coastline will bend more parallel to the coast and speed up. This effect is noticeable on the north coast of France in strong nor'easterlies. The

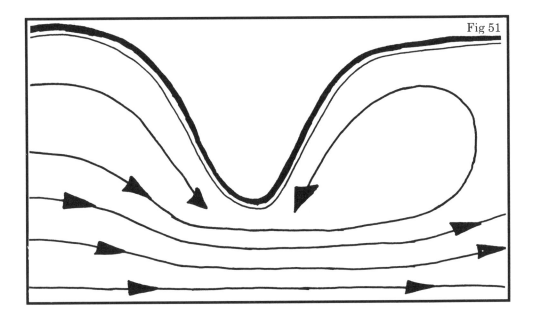

Fig 51

wind can also funnel through gaps and accelerate like a tidal stream, the Dover Strait being a good example in sou'westerlies and nor'easterlies (see figure 51).

Winds can also be diverted in a vertical plane over a high coastline. Onshore winds tend to rise over steep cliffs before reaching them, leaving an area of calm close in; while offshore winds take time to regain sea level, also leaving an area of calm close under the cliffs, or even a light onshore back eddy. In rivers and estuaries the wind can be influenced greatly by such things as trees, tall buildings, hills and even large anchored ships. These can all cause gusts, eddies and flat patches that are not at all easy to predict. Their likelihood, however, can put the pilot on guard so that he avoids getting into a position (when perhaps under sail with no motor) where he could lose control of his boat.

Poor Visibility

Although fog is the most serious and most obvious cause of this, it is important to appreciate that heavy rain can cause a dangerous reduction of visibility when in coastal waters. Even drizzle and low, dark cloud can reduce visibility noticeably when you are trying to pick up isolated marks a few miles off a low, featureless coast. At dusk the difficulties in such a situation, when you are perhaps surrounded by buoyed sandbanks that cannot be approached closely, can be almost as bad as those caused by fog.

Very rough weather can generate sufficient spray and spume to also reduce visibility. In conjunction with waves obscuring the lookout's vision intermittently, and the lethargy brought on by rough weather, often the end result can be seriously impaired visibility. Blind pilotage techniques may be required

just as urgently in these conditions as they are in real fog.

Fog

Real fog, however, is almost certainly the most dangerous of conditions for the coastal pilot, especially in a small boat without electronic aids such as Decca and radar. Special blind pilotage techniques (see chapter 10) must be honed to perfection for safe pilotage in thick fog, especially around the busier and more dangerous parts of the coast.

Three different types of fog are likely to be experienced in coastal waters and they are all caused by the same basic conditions: warm, moist air being cooled to below its dew point. The dew point of air is the lowest temperature at which it can hold the water vapour that it carries. As it falls below its dew point, the water vapour condenses out as fog. Three different situations commonly produce this effect, and as a result the fogs caused by these situations have quite different properties. It is thus most important to be able to recognise what type of fog you are in, as that can have a major influence on the way in which you deal with it.

Sea Fog: this is the worst as it is the most difficult to predict and the most reluctant to disperse, but it is the one likely to be mentioned in the shipping forecast. It is caused by warm, moist air passing over cold sea, and it will not disperse until the weather pattern changes so as to bring in a different –

Photo 14 (overleaf) *High headlands like this one on the north coast of Jersey can cause much interference to the wind, especially when it blows along the coast.*

drier or cooler – airstream. It is common in the Western Approaches to the English Channel in spring when warm, moist sou'westerly winds blow in over a sea still cold from the winter. It is also common, and extremely persistent at times, on the North Sea coast of Britain in easterly winds, due to colder water on the British side of the North Sea causing the air, moist from its trip across warmer sea to the east, to fall below its dew point.

In borderline conditions sea fog can be most unpredictable, especially in areas of strong tides such as North Brittany where cold water can suddenly swirl up from the depths and cause often widespread patches and banks. It can also persist in very strong winds and be blown from a sea area where it is forecast into a neighbouring one in which it is not. Sea fog must be treated with the greatest respect.

Frontal Fog: this is basically the same as sea fog, with the same causes, but it occurs only in bands along warm weather fronts where the right conditions prevail. The moment the front passes over, a different airstream is drawn in and the fog disperses rapidly.

Radiation Fog: this is a rather different phenomenon and much easier to cope with. It is essentially a land fog that forms at night and then pours down river valleys and estuaries to spread, perhaps five or ten miles, out to sea in the early morning. It is caused after a hot day when the land cools off, thus cooling the air close to it below its dew point. Fog forms near to the ground, usually in dips, hollows and valleys where the cold air collects, and then flows out to sea. The sun next day heats up the fog and evaporates it, usually by mid-morning. In winter, however, when a thick layer

of fog builds up during the long cold night, the weak sun next day may not burn it up. The next night the process begins anew, but with a head start as it were, and the next day's fog will be thicker than the previous. In this sort of situation thick radiation fog can persist for some days. In summer the layer of fog is usually quite shallow, often so shallow that you can see over it from the top of the mast (see chapter 10).

Other Hazards

Buoys marking fishing gear can be a real nuisance, especially at night and if you are under power. There is not much useful advice that one can give other than to avoid, if possible, areas where concentrations of markers are likely to be found. These may well be noted in the Pilot Book. Slack Low Water is the riskiest time, when the surplus line is likely to be floating about on the surface and lying in all directions. As the stream begins to run so the lines will lie along the direction of it, and gradually sink. At High Water springs even the buoy itself may be submerged. If you can afford it, one of those rope cutters that bolt onto the prop shaft may well prove a sound investment, especially for a powerboat operating in areas infested with such gear.

Unattended drift nets create a similar hazard, and in some places these can be a serious problem at certain times of the year. It is a great deal more difficult to clear one of these from a prop or rudder than it is to cut away or clear a single rope. Pilot Books will often advise on the likelihood of encountering concentrations of such things, and the periods when they are usually in evidence.

Shipping, of course, can be a serious hazard in coastal waters and this problem is dealt with in detail in chapter 12.

8
Piloting by Eye

Navigating purely by eye is not such a casual, offhand business as may at first appear. The experienced pilot in truth is actually shooting mental fixes in his head, and if the type of fix is chosen carefully it can be at least as accurate as a compass fix plotted on the chart; in certain circumstances it can actually be more accurate.

More to the point, however, is the fact that all too often there just is not time for shooting and plotting traditional fixes when negotiating pilotage waters, so the experienced pilot will develop his eyeball fixing to a fine art. Much of the time he will use transits (see chapter 6), but there will be occasions on which he needs a more precise actual position, or perhaps more often an accurate distance off. This latter is frequently essential when passing headlands with off-lying dangers, and there are several ways in which it can be found quickly and without recourse to complex chart plotting.

Distance Off by Eye

The simplest and quickest, but least accurate way of doing this is to look at the object you want a distance from and gauge its range from experience.

Inevitably this is fraught with risks – although its reliability increases considerably with practice and regular use – but there are certain guidelines and clues that can help you to gauge distance purely by eye.

To begin again with the quickest and least accurate, it is possible to gauge a rough distance off buoys or people on a beach by the way their appearances alter with their range. For example, large navigation buoys generally become visible with the naked eye as vague blobs at about two miles from the deck of a small boat. At one mile the shape can be verified and at half a mile usually they can be clearly identified by shape, colour and topmark. With binoculars these distances will be roughly doubled.

People standing on a shore can also provide a similarly rough distance off, as can the clarity of shore-side buildings and so on. Trees and houses can just about be seen at four miles; windows and doors at two miles; people and traffic as blobs at one mile, and identifiable at half a mile. It is worth studying what can be seen at certain distances for yourself, and building up a useful dossier in the back of the logbook.

Distance Off by Instrument

A far more accurate estimate of distance off can be found by using even the most rudimentary of measuring instruments. Those of you who were in the Boy Scouts in childhood will remember the markings on the Scout's staff that enabled it to be used as a simple range finder. The same thing can be done from the deck of a boat using an ordinary ruler.

If the ruler is held upright 60cm from the eye, then one centimetre of it will represent a vertical angle of one degree. By sighting the ruler against a lighthouse or whatever of known height, its lower end aligned with sea-level at the base, the angle subtended by the object can be read off in centimetres, each one representing one degree. This angle can then be entered into the relevant table in an Almanac to give your distance off an object of that height. Even quicker (but less accurate) is to simply divide the charted height of the object in feet by the measured height in millimetres, to give an immediate distance off in nautical miles (see figure 52).

The same thing can be done more accurately still with a vertical sextant angle (see chapter 6). Even with a simple ruler you should bear in mind the points made there about the height of a light.

Dipping Ranges

Because of the curvature of the Earth lights will pop up over the horizon as you approach within a certain distance of them. If you know your height of eye above sea-level and the height of the light above sea-level you can quite easily calculate the range at which a particular light will pop up. This is known as the dipping range, as this is the range at which the light will dip below the horizon if you are going away from it (see figure 53). If there is any low cloud about you can usually see the 'loom' of the light (glow in the sky) some time before it actually shows as a light on the horizon. This gives a very convenient indication of the light's position, often at ranges considerably in excess of the dipping range.

Fig 52

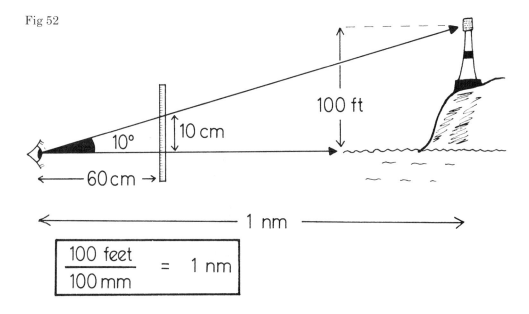

$$\frac{100 \text{ feet}}{100 \text{ mm}} = 1 \text{ nm}$$

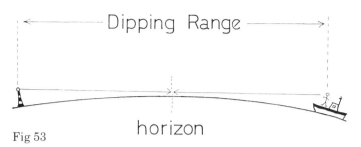

Fig 53

horizon

These dipping ranges can be especially useful when approaching a landfall as they give a quick and simple distance off. The dipping range crossed with a compass bearing of the light will also give a useful, if approximate, initial landfall fix. Nautical Almanacs usually contain tables of dipping ranges to save you having to make the calculations yourself. Simply enter them with your height of eye and the height of the light and read off the range (see chapters 3 and 6).

A similar effect to this can be experienced with town or city lights ashore, although the navigational usefulness is much more approximate. The loom of a big city's lights can often be seen at great ranges, and can provide a handy guide to your rough position. If these lights are on the coast you may be able to get an idea of your distance off from

their dipping range as the loom turns into actual lights.

Doubling the Angle on the Bow

This is a useful type of running fix that gives your distance off a headland without having to plot anything on the chart. Measure the relative bearing off the bow of a distant headland or lighthouse with the hand-bearing compass and read the log. Then keep checking the increase in this bearing as you close with the object, until the bearing doubles, then read the log again. The distance you have travelled over the ground between the bearings will be equal to your distance from the object. In the absence of leeway or tidal stream, this will be equal to the difference between the log readings (see figure 54). If allowance has to be made for drift, then the quickness and

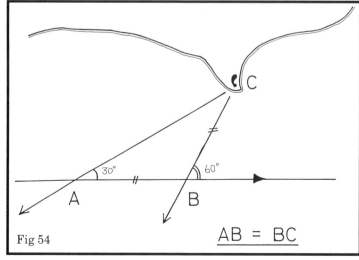

Fig 54

AB = BC

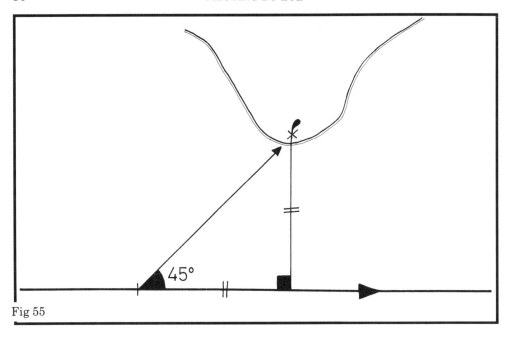

Fig 55

simplicity of the method is rather lost, as you will then have to plot the drift on the chart in order to calculate the true distance run over the ground (see chapter 6).

The 'four-point bearing' is a special case which will give your distance off a headland when it is abeam. Take a log reading when the headland bears 45° off the bow, and again when it is abeam. The distance run over the ground between these readings is then equal to your distance abeam of the object. This can even be done without a compass if you mark on the guardrail a point that represents a relative bearing of 45° when viewed from the normal steering position in the cockpit (see figure 55).

Distance to Pass Abeam of Object

Of course there will be occasions on which, if the distance abeam is wrong, then finding so when the object is abeam will be rather too late! Fortu-

nately, there are certain pairs of angles which will predict your distance abeam of the headland before you get there: the distance run between the two relative bearings being equal to the distance you will pass abeam of the headland (assuming steady course steered and no tidal stream or leeway). These pairs of angles are listed in figure 56. It is worth keeping this list in the navigator's notebook for quick reference.

A particularly useful pair of angles is 30° and 60°, as these can provide both the direct distance from the headland and also the projected distance you will pass abeam of it. The distance run between them is your direct distance off, while ⅞ of this distance is that at which you will pass abeam of it. Mathematicians should be able to work out why.

Angles of 22½° and 45° produce a similar result; ⁷⁄₁₀ of the run being equal to the distance you will pass abeam. Unless, however, you have a compass reading in points, so giving 2

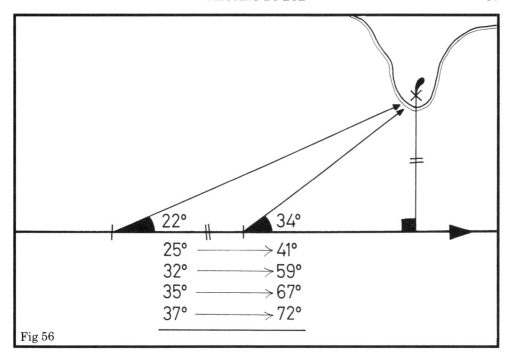

22°   34°
25° ———————→ 41°
32° ———————→ 59°
35° ———————→ 67°
37° ———————→ 72°

Fig 56

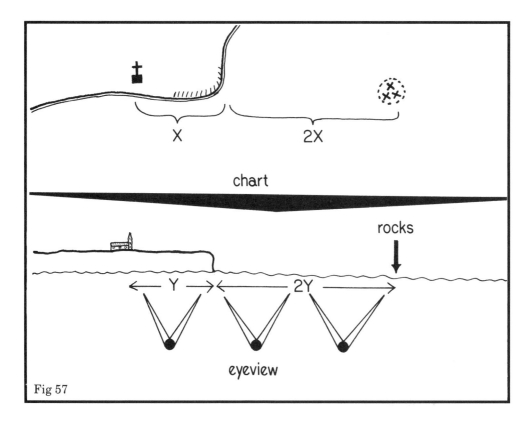

X   2X

chart

rocks

Y   2Y

eyeview

Fig 57

points and 4 points, you will find it difficult to measure accurately to ½°.

It is most important with all these running fixes that you maintain a steady and accurate course between the bearings, so that distance run on the log is correct and the relative bearings are precise.

Position of an Off-lying Danger

In suitable conditions the position of, say, a submerged rock off a headland can be ascertained fairly simply as shown in figure 57. On the chart set your dividers to the distance between the headland and a prominent object, such as a lighthouse, that lies just inside it. Then step off this distance from the headland out to the charted danger so as to measure how much further outside the headland the danger is compared to the distance inside of the lighthouse. Then go on deck and set the dividers to the actual distance you can see between the headland and the prominent visible object. Stepping them out from the headland the same number of times you did on the chart will then indicate where the danger lies.

Measuring Distance on the Horizon

Rough horizontal distances can also be measured as shown in figures 58 and 59. The first employs a similar technique to that of a camera's rangefinder – using

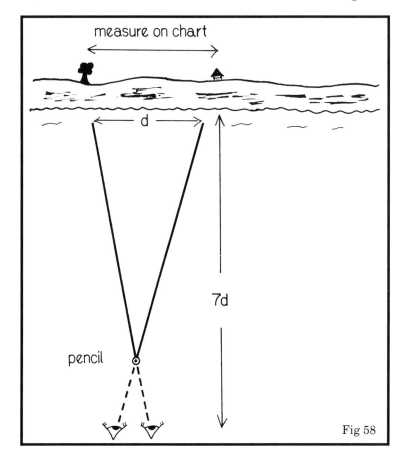

measure on chart

d

7d

pencil

Fig 58

the horizontal separation of the eyes to measure range. Hold a pencil at arm's length before the eyes and align it with a distant object, keeping one eye closed. Then open that eye and close the other. Due to the change in viewpoint the pencil will appear to move sideways, and it will move about ⅐ or ⅛ of the range of the object. Experiment with known situations to find just how far your eyes cause the pencil to jump. It may also be worth trying this back to front in order to find a range when the horizontal distances of an object from a number of other nearby features can be determined.

In figure 59 the horizontal distance at a horizon three miles away (approximately that as seen from a small boat), can be measured roughly from the angles subtended by the fist and the open hand held at arm's length. The accuracy of this measurement can be improved considerably if you plot it all out on paper beforehand. Check from height of eye tables and your actual height of eye the distance of the horizon from the deck of your boat; measure the distance of your outstretched hand from your eyes; measure the width of your fist and your open fingers. Then plot this out to see the precise angles represented and the distances covered at the horizon.

Clearance under Bridges

It is particularly useful to be able to measure by eye if you have to pass regularly under a bridge with limited

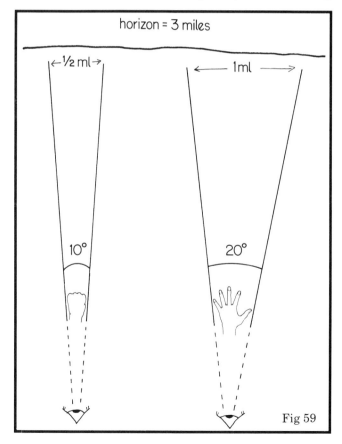

Fig 59

clearance. When viewed from the cockpit at a particular range, the height of the under part of the bridge will be proportional to the height at which it is seen to cross the mast (see figure 60). A simple calculation will enable you to mark the mast at the lowest height the bridge should cross it in order to provide safe clearance, when viewed from a specific distance – when a prominent object is abeam, for example.

Echo-sounder and Leadline

Soundings can often be used to great effect when piloting by eye, as they can be taken very quickly and do not require plotting. Good, sharp depth contours running along the coast will give surprisingly accurate distances off, although these are best used as clearing lines (see next section). Arming the lead will enable you to inspect the nature of

Photo 15 *A typical headland of the type likely to have off-lying submerged rocks. The dividers technique will enable you quickly and simply to gauge their position, comparing their distance off with the distance between headland and lighthouse.*

the seabed, which could be useful in certain situations.

Regular soundings with suitable contours can also give helpful warning of approaching landfall as contours are crossed. Soundings really come into their own, however, when piloting in fog, and this will be covered fully in chapter 10.

Clearing Lines

These provide extremely useful and simple ways of keeping a boat out of dangerous waters when negotiating restricted

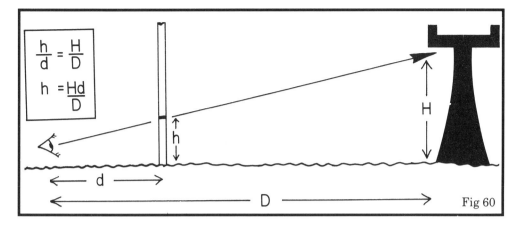

$$\frac{h}{d} = \frac{H}{D}$$

$$h = \frac{Hd}{D}$$

Fig 60

places, such as harbour entrances, narrow channels, sandbanks, rocks, etc. In principle, a clearing line is any line that runs clear to one side of a danger and can be followed by a boat. It can be a compass bearing, depth contour, Decca lane, radar range, vertical danger angle (giving distance off), sectored light, and so on. The best and most accurate type of clearing line, however, is the transit. Let us look at the use of this first.

Transits

A transit is simply a line joining two fixed objects. As long as a helmsman steers to keep the far object directly behind the near one at all times he can be certain that his boat is on that line. It is the one type of clearing line that cannot be affected by any kind of error or inaccuracy, other than the selection of the wrong objects, so should always be chosen, if possible, in preference to any other. The identity of the objects can be checked by comparing the compass heading, when directly on line, with that shown or measured on the chart.

Transits are often marked on charts to indicate the safe course to enter harbour or to clear a danger, and their bearings are given in degrees True as

viewed from seaward (see figure 61). Before checking the identification of the marks this bearing must be converted to degrees Compass, if you use the main steering compass. This is a very quick and easy way of taking a bearing if you are short-handed; simply aim the boat at the mark and read off the course from

Fig 61

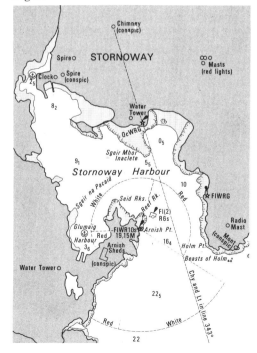

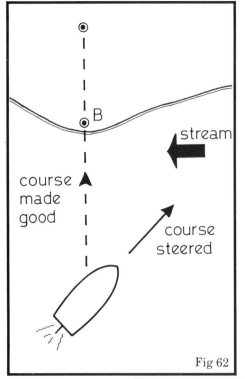

stream

course
made
good

course
steered

Fig 62

the steering compass. Apply deviation
and/or variation as explained in chapter 5 in order to produce a Magnetic or
True bearing.

It is important to realise that in
conditions of leeway or cross-tides the
heading of the boat as you progress will
not be that of the transit, as you may
have to crab sideways in order to remain
on the line (see figure 62). In such conditions the bearing check may have to be
made with the hand-bearing compass,
which will give degrees Magnetic.

If you begin drifting off to one side
of the transit then a bold alteration of
course should be made – towards the
near mark – in order to regain the line
as quickly as possible. Remember that
the line itself leads clear of danger and
the moment you get off it, by however
little, you immediately lose the certainty of safety. You must avoid the
temptation to edge back gradually as it

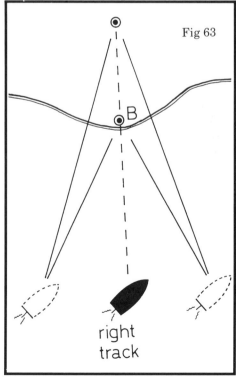

Fig 63

right
track

is not easy to assess how far off the line you are while doing so (see figure 63).

These marked transits, if they lead into harbour, are often referred to as leading marks. Sometimes they will utilise existing features – churches, trees, edge of cliff, white house, etc – but often they will consist of specially erected structures, perhaps coloured and with shaped topmarks. In all but

the smallest of harbours they will also usually carry lights, when they may be referred to in the Pilot Book or on the chart as leading lights (see figure 64).

Unmarked Transits

It is very often possible to find your own transits on a chart for leading clear of dangers. A particularly useful type is

Fig 64

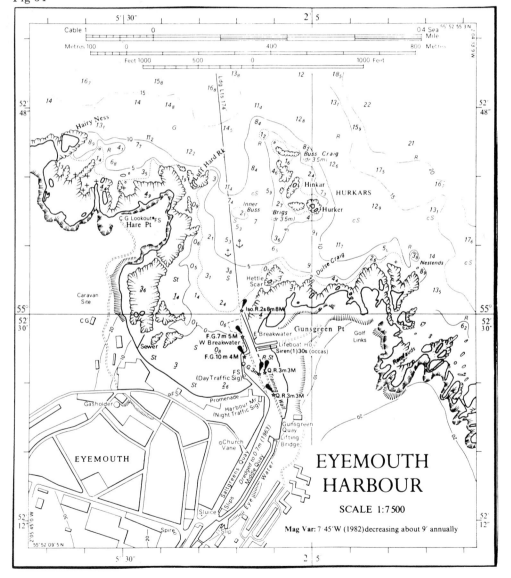

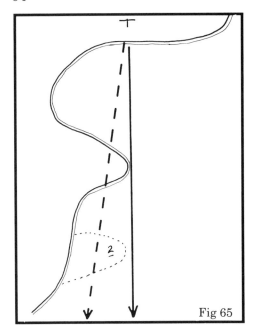

Fig 65

Gauging Progress by Transits

Transits viewed to the side of the boat provide excellent indication of progress over the ground, especially in strong tides and light winds when this progress might be very small. Any number of home-made transits may be utilised for this, and overall movement can be assessed quite accurately by observing transits both ahead and abeam. When using transits for this purpose you have only to remember that your movement over the ground is in the direction that the rear mark moves.

This operation can also be carried out using single shore marks in transit with part of the boat. If you align a part of the boat with a buoy or shore object and hold your eye fixed in the same position then the relative movement of the boat mark and the shore mark will indicate your movement over the ground. In this case, however, your movement is in the direction that the near (boat) mark moves in relation to the far one. If the two remain in line then progress is either nil or directly towards or away from the shore mark, just as it is when a conventional transit remains aligned.

Clearing Bearings

These are compass bearings of marks ashore that lead clear of particular dangers. Because of possible errors in the compass and in the reading of it they are not as accurate as transits, although more versatile as they can be used with single marks. Some examples can be seen in figure 66. The same comments in the previous section about cross-streams and leeway apply even more strongly to clearing bearings and it is most important to work out carefully which way you are drifting off line as the bearing changes (see figure 67).

A compass bearing on a mark can

what I call the open transit. With this type the two objects in line, very often a structure or isolated rock aligned with a cliff edge or similar, leads very close to the edge of danger and you simply sail to keep the far one 'open' of the near one – ie, visible. Often the far one is hidden behind the near one when you are on line for the danger, so keeping it open to the side leads you clear (see figure 65).

Another useful home-made transit can be employed when steering a compass course towards a buoy or beacon if there is land in the background. The moment you line the mark up on your course you look for a conspicuous mark ashore that is in line with it – tree, house, fold in the hills, etc – and steer on that transit instead of the compass course. This will also give some indication of tidal stream effect or leeway as the compass course alters in order to maintain the transit.

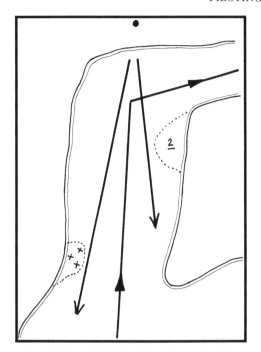

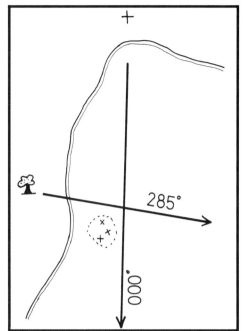

Fig 66

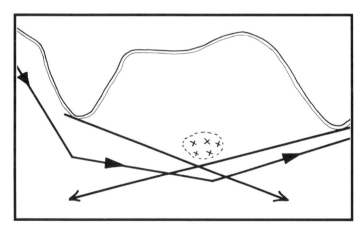

also be used in order to run in on a direct line towards it. In this case you simply steer to remain on the bearing constantly (using the hand-bearing compass) instead of merely keeping to one side of it.

Back Bearings

When sailing away from a mark, such as a buoy or harbour entrance, a similar technique can be employed using a bearing astern (back bearing). Plot from the mark the course required to clear the dangers then maintain the mark on the reciprocal of this using the hand-bearing compass. Course corrections to allow for tidal stream and leeway will be back-to-front and rather confusing, so it pays to practise this so as to get the feel of how to correct. If in doubt, plot it all out on the chart to see which way the bearing will change as you drift to one side or the other.

Depth Contours

In certain situations these can be extremely useful clearing lines, especially when a wavering course is required to weave in and out of a series of dangers such as sandbanks, but they need to be used with some circumspection. A safe type of clearing depth contour can be seen in figure 68. The contour is reasonably even, without violent twists that could make it difficult to follow, and without ambiguous sections of deep water that could make it impossible to be certain which side of the line you are on. The bottom shelves steeply enough to make the contour sharp and clearly defined. A navigator could safely follow this contour right round the headland and into the safe water of the estuary whatever the conditions of visibility.

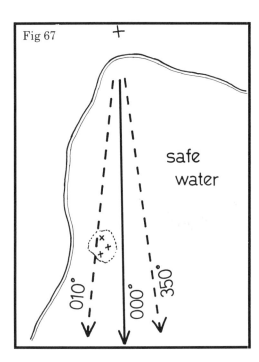

Fig 67

safe water

010°   000°   350°

This is a particularly useful type of clearing line when navigating in fog, and it will be discussed in more detail in chapter 10.

A simpler clearing line is a coastal contour that merely serves to indicate the outer limits of navigational dangers. If you keep in deeper water than the contour while coasting you will remain at all times clear of those inshore dangers. Remember to reduce the actual depth to soundings by subtracting the current tidal height, and make sure you know whether your echo-sounder reads the depth below transducer, keel or surface. What you need, of course, is the depth below the surface.

More specialised uses of depth contours, and sounding generally will also be found in chapter 11.

Clearing Ranges

These are useful for maintaining a fixed distance clear of a coastline or for passing a set distance off a headland, for example, and there are various ways of measuring them. They are commonly employed when navigating blind by radar and the precise techniques are explained in chapter 10.

A more traditional type of clearing range is the 'vertical danger angle'. When approaching a headland or lighthouse and requiring to keep a certain distance off, the navigator can set on his sextant an angle that when subtended by the vertical height of the lighthouse will indicate the required distance off (see chapter 6). Then he only need ensure that the height of the lighthouse as seen in the sextant remains always smaller than the limiting height.

The ruler technique can be used in the same way (see earlier section on *Distance Off by Instrument*).

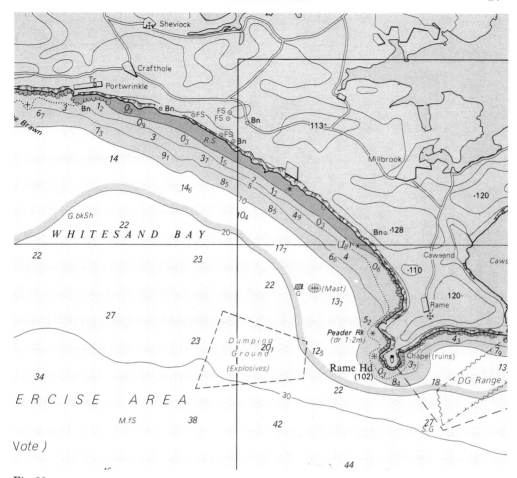

Vote)

Fig 68

Sectored Lights

Lights showing different colours over certain arcs of visibility are often to be found in the approaches to harbours, or projected from lighthouses to cover areas of dangerous water. Commonly a sectored leading light will show a red light to port of the entry line and a green one to starboard. The safe entry line is usually marked with a narrow white sector. However, the chart should be checked carefully for the precise characteristics, and also for a mark or light indicating the safe point at which the white sector may be left for the final entry into the harbour (see figure 69).

Lighthouses often show, in addition to an all-round main light, a fixed red light over a particular sector that covers, perhaps, a dangerous shallow bank. Others may be fully sectored like leading lights, but showing various colours and characteristics over sectors that may indicate a number of different dangers. The chart must be studied carefully to ascertain these sectors and the dangers they indicate.

Other Clearing Lines

Many other features can be used, with varying degrees of accuracy, for leading a vessel clear of dangers. Decca lanes are frequently used by fishermen as clearing lines, but they are of use only to the yachtsman who possesses a Decca set giving raw hyperbolic co-ordinates and an overprinted Decca chart.

Much less accurate, but potentially useful in certain circumstances, are such guides as tide-lines, breaking surf along the edge of a bank, the change in water colour along the side of a channel and so on (see next section).

Observing the Water

The behaviour of the water itself, due to such influences as tidal eddies, shal-

lows, and so on, can be a very useful, if approximate, guide to position. This is discussed in some detail in chapter 11, where it is applied to the business of keeping out of trouble when piloting without a chart. The techniques are, of

Fig 69 *In this example a wide white sector covers the safe approach, flanked by red sectors marking the danger limits either side. When a narrow white sector marks a leading line the starboard danger light is very often green, so as to match the buoyage system lights. Note the different ranges for white and red lights given in the light characteristic; the ranges being given in the same order as the colours.*

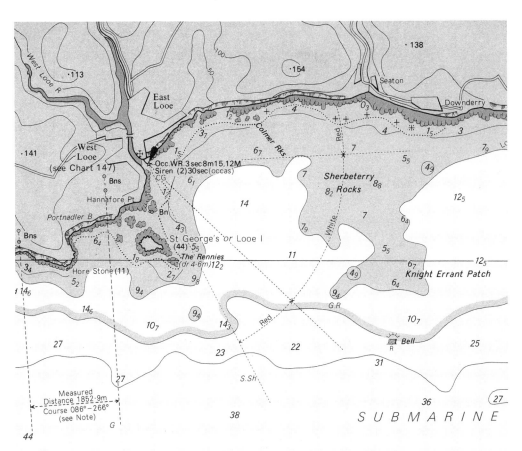

Photo 16 *A deep-drafted vessel such as this tug will invariably lie to the tidal stream when moored or anchored. Light motor cruisers with a lot of top-hamper, or shallow-draft yachts with much rigging will tend to be affected much more by the wind.*

course, equally useful as a general guide to or a check on position when piloting by eye with a chart. Besides generally indicating places of danger to be avoided, or deep water channels to be followed, signs in the water can also indicate the whereabouts of specific, charted places that can help in fixing the position of the boat.

Overfalls and races are certainly not places you should be stumbling through unaware of your position, as they can create very dangerous conditions for small boats. In reasonable weather, however, the turbulence caused by such phenomena can often be seen at a sufficient distance to mark their positions and help to check yours. Binoculars are useful for this as you do not want to get too close to any but the most minor of races, even in quiet weather.

Steep breaking waves are often seen over off-lying banks in otherwise deep water, and this can give an accurate indication of the position of the bank. Rocks close to the surface often show an area of smooth, swirling water close by them when a strong tidal stream is running. This will generally be downstream of the rock, but other influences can conspire to cause the upwelling of the swirl to appear some way from the rock that is causing it. Such a position indicator must be treated with the greatest caution.

Checking a Tidal Stream

A very convenient way to check the precise strength and direction of a tidal stream is simply to stem the tide and hold yourself stationary alongside a buoy. The reciprocal of your compass heading will give its direction and your log, speedometer or Dutchman's Log will give its speed. This is particularly useful in conditions of poor visibility.

Less accurate but very useful judgements of tidal stream strength and direction can be made by observing the water flowing past buoys, moored boats and so on, as you sail past. Make a point of sailing close to such things, if convenient, so that you can check the tidal stream at every opportunity. These guides are especially useful when negotiating harbours and rivers, where tidal streams may vary considerably in both strength and direction over very short distances, due to the influence of banks, bends, obstructions, shallows, and so on (see chapter 4).

Tidal stream direction can be judged from a distance by observing how anchored and moored boats are lying to their cables, but account must be taken of wind effect in all but very light breezes.

9

Harbours and Anchorages

This is the final part of your pilotage and it can be fraught with difficulties, many of them not strictly navigational. A considerable amount of information is presented to the navigator on entering a busy commercial port, for example, and it is not always easy to sort out the essential from the inessential. A night entry can be particularly difficult due to the plethora of lights winking at you from buoys, beacons, leading lights and so on. Sorting these out can be a problem at times, especially when relative distances are distorted by varying light intensities; powerful distant lights appearing much closer than they are, and weak near ones seeming to be far distant.

It is essential to be especially well organised for approaching and entering a busy commercial harbour at night.

Preparing the Boat

This is really a matter of seamanship rather than pilotage, but the two tend to become closely intertwined at times like this. Only if you know that the boat is thoroughly prepared for all eventualities can you properly concentrate as you should on the pilotage aspects of entering harbour.

The basic object of this exercise is to check and prepare all the items of equipment that might possibly be needed in a hurry while negotiating the harbour and looking for your berth. The anchor should be cleared away ready for instant use in emergency, or in case you need to stop somewhere to await entry or berthing. All mooring warps and fenders should be sorted out and put on deck in roughly the right places ready for going alongside, which you may have to do quickly due to a sudden change of plan.

If you are under sail then make all your engine checks (oil, water, etc) before entering, then run up the engine to normal operating temperature, check all gauges and systems, gears and throttle, so that on entering you are certain everything will work properly. Then leave the engine ticking over in neutral so that it is immediately available should it be required. If the batteries need charging you can run at a fast tickover and get them charged during the entry to save having to run the engine when you want peace and quiet in the berth.

At night make a final check on your navigation lights, torches and spotlights before entry.

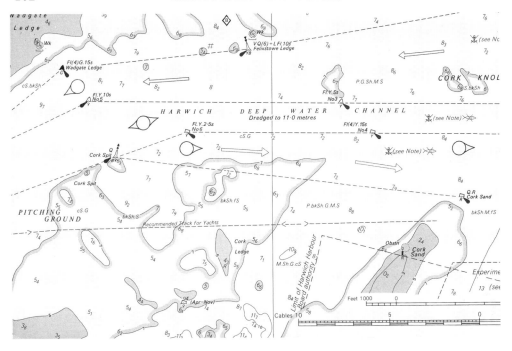

Fig 70 *The recommended yacht channel is south of the deep water channel, marked in very small lettering. Arrows show the direction of traffic in the outer commercial vessel channels and the pointed circles are reporting positions: vessels report passing these positions. Listening to the Harbour Control channel on VHF will tell you where the vessels are. Note that the deep water channel is two-way, for very large ships only.*

Preparing the Entry

This is basically the same routine that was described in chapter 2 when we prepared for entering pilotage waters, except that more detail will be required. It is particularly important to know where you can safely go during the approach and entry in case you have to make a detour to avoid large ships, fleets of dinghies and so on. Busy ports may have special entry channels for yachts and small craft and you must ensure that you know where they are and how they are marked (see figure 70).

The navigator's notebook is especially useful here as it can be filled with all the essential details that you might need to refer to quickly. Work out times and heights of tide and enter them hourly for the duration of your entry, then you do not have suddenly to make mental tidal calculations if you decide, or are forced, to alter your berthing plans. If you need to go well out of the channel to avoid anything a quick glance in the notebook will tell you instantly the height of tide at that moment, thus helping you to work out where you can safely go.

List all the buoys and features that you should pass during the approach and entry, then cross them off in the book as you pass them. This is particularly useful when negotiating a long, frequently-buoyed channel, as it avoids the risk of suddenly forgetting which buoy you have passed. Note places where you need to alter course, with guiding transits, bearings or buoys that

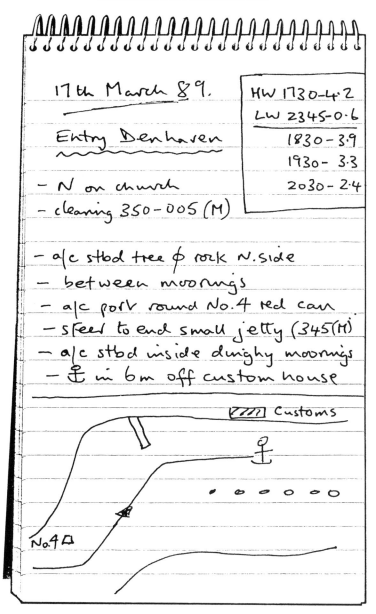

17th March 89.

HW 1730-4·2
LW 2345-0·6
    1830-3·9
    1930- 3·3
    2030- 2·4

Entry Denhaven

- N on church
- clearing 350-005 (M)

- a/c stbd tree φ rock N.side
- between moorings
- a/c port round No.4 red can
- steer to end small jetty (345(M)
- a/c stbd inside dinghy moorings
- ⚓ in 6m off custom house

Customs

No.4

Fig 71

indicate the place, and cross these off as you pass. This way you keep clear track of your progress without having to rush back and forth to the logbook and chart every two minutes. In poor visibility the times of passing buoys, etc, should be noted so that you always have, in effect, a timed position to refer to if you start getting lost or confused. A simple sketch chart of the entry and harbour will be found useful, marked with the main buoys and leadings marks that you indend using and with your projected route pencilled in. Note on it also any tidal stream anomalies warned of in the Pilot Book or chart (see figure 71).

Finding a Berth

This is usually the most difficult decision facing a newcomer to cruising, and often continues to remain so for the more experienced skipper. With the proliferation of yacht marinas these days this problem is diminishing (assuming you have the wherewithal to pay the charges and the inclination to enter one), but it nevertheless, for various reasons, requires some thought.

The easiest situation is a moderate sized harbour with VHF Port Control: you can simply call them up on their working channel and ask for a berth. Most harbours are very helpful, if only because it is in their interests to get all boats moored safely out of the way as quickly as possible.

Probably the most difficult is the river or bay marked with an anchor to indicate good anchorage, and described by the Pilot Book as being an excellent anchorage. Tempted by all this you sail smartly in and discover – all too often in a narrow river with a following gale and sluicing flood tide – that the place is jammed solid with moorings! It can be quite a task finding a berth in such places, especially at night, and the wise skipper approaches such anchorages with some caution, especially if turning and getting out again could be troublesome (see figure 72).

Do not be afraid to let go the anchor temporarily in the nearest space while you take a good look round, by dinghy if necessary. For a very brief stop like this you need only enough room to lie the way the other boats are lying and you can hang on a short scope; there

Fig 72

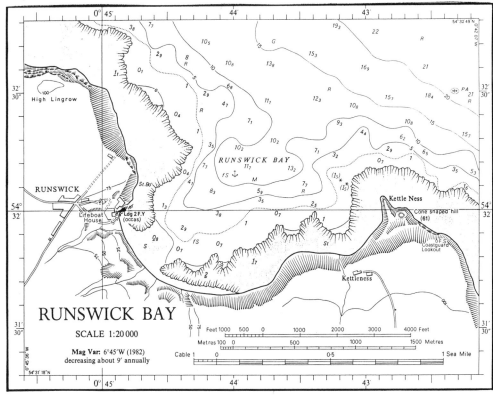

is no need to provide swinging room to cover all eventualities. Do take care, however, not to let go across a mooring chain. Most are laid up and down the stream, but occasionally you will find them across it. The Pilot Book should advise if this is the case.

Many places have visitors' moorings these days and you can normally lie to one of these if you can find one. The Pilot Book may mention their existence but not their positions. Look on the side of the buoy where you will generally find a note of the maximum weight of boat permitted, and perhaps a large 'V' to denote 'visitors' mooring'. If there is nothing, then haul up the buoy and inspect the size of the riser chain; if it is as big as your anchor chain then the mooring is

Photo 17 This is fairly typical of what you usually find in a recommended anchorage. It is not always easy for even an experienced skipper to find a decent berth in such a place.

probably heavy enough. While the buoy is up inspect the shackle attaching it to the riser for chafe or corrosion, as this is the most likely place for wear. Consult the harbourmaster or local yacht club as soon as possible to confirm that you may stay on the buoy for the duration of your visit.

Drying Berths

Berths that dry out at Low Water are often available, particularly in small harbours, but they must be used with some care. There are two basic types: the hard berth and the mud berth. A boat will stand on top of the former and sink into the latter, and both contain many potential problems.

First, the height of tide required for getting in, and out again must be calculated accurately. Such berths should, ideally, be entered about two hours before High Water, and only when the tides are making up towards springs. That way you give yourself plenty of time to get settled in the berth before the tide begins falling, and you can be sure that there will be sufficient water to get you out the next day or whenever. If the berth only partially dries, then these constraints are obviously not nearly so critical.

If the berth is tight for depth, however, you must also take careful note of factors that might affect the height of the tide, such as atmospheric pressure, tidal surges, wind strength and direction, and so on (see chapter 4). If you chance your arm a little in a tight berth and some of these factors conspire to cut the height the next day, you could be there for a fortnight.

The presence of wind and swell in an exposed harbour must also be considered, as great strains can be exerted on a boat if she pounds on the bottom in a swell while grounding or lifting in a hard berth. This is not so much of a problem in a mud berth, although bad weather like that could cause the boat to settle to one side of the hole she has dug. As the mud in the hole will be much softer than that on the edges, she will then list towards the hole. This is not likely to be serious unless it causes her to lean on a neighbouring boat, or to tangle her mast and rigging in its. You should line up a couple of transits ahead and astern while properly in the hole so that warps

can be adjusted, if necessary, on the next ebb to ensure that she regains the hole when the tide goes.

If possible, any drying berth, be it hard or mud, should be inspected beforehand at Low Water for obstructions or rubbish that might cause you to lie awkwardly, or even could poke through the bottom of the boat. Hard patches in a mud berth could put great strains on a boat if she lies across one, and a soft patch in a hard berth can be disastrous if you stand on legs and the one you lean on falls into it.

The Use of VHF Radio

This is a very handy piece of equipment when entering all but the smallest of harbours. Although often touted as a safety aid, in my view the major benefit of VHF radio is for entering harbour and organising a berth. Most large ports have a Port Operations Frequency on which all the traffic control is conducted. By listening to this frequency you can learn about the big ship movements, any dangers to shipping, dredging operations and so on that are taking place in and around the harbour.

You can also call up on this channel to request information about such matters, as well as details of berthing arrangements, tidal times and heights, locking and bridge opening times and operational details, etc. Many large ports will have more than one channel for these operations and they will be noted in the Almanac. The main channel, on which all broadcast information and most traffic control are conducted will be marked in bold type. Sometimes the harbourmaster's launch will operate on one of the subsidiary channels and you may often find it useful to communicate directly with him for certain things, rather than go through the Port Control itself.

Most marinas these days can be contacted (usually only during normal working hours,) on VHF, British marinas having specially designated marina channels. These are Channel 37 (known as M) and Channel 80, but certain areas use other channels. Check with the Pilot Book or Almanac, or with the main Harbour Control if the marina is in the area of a large harbour. Marinas are not normally licensed to transmit on any channel other than these, so do not waste your time and other people's patience by calling them on Channel 16.

Local Regulations

Many ports have local regulations concerning such things as entry signals, speed limits, restrictions on entering under sail, manoeuvring sound signals, and so on. These will be found in the Pilot Book covering the harbour, and they should be studied carefully if you are not to make a fool of yourself, or even possibly get into serious trouble if you are faced with a big ship whose movements you should, but do not understand.

In some places – such as North America – international buoyage systems, navigation lights and even rule of the road may change on passing into harbour limits, so it is extremely important that you study Pilot Books and charts very carefully for all such local irregularities. Inland waterways, especially, tend to have their own rules; sometimes in addition to, and sometimes instead of, international conventions. Make sure you understand them before entry, and that you know at what point during your entry they come into operation.

Harbour Entry Signals

A serious attempt is currently under way to rationalise all harbour entry signals into an internationally accepted code. Details will be found in appendix 4. In the meantime, local signals must be checked assiduously before entry. Bear in mind, however, that many of these signals are really applicable only to large vessels, and often there will be subsidiary signals or exemptions for small boats.

As well as controlling entry and exit so that vessels keep clear of one another in restricted spaces, these harbour signals often indicate dangers involved in entry. Some harbours may close during certain stages of the tide in onshore gales, for example, because of the risks involved in entering at those times. Drying harbours may have signals indicating the depth in the harbour, commercial ports may have one-way traffic when large ships are entering or leaving, and so on. These signals are not mere red tape, so pay attention to them. Some very busy yacht harbours in the Solent also close at about four o'clock on a summer Friday because they are full.

Anchorages

Anchoring in open bays, river estuaries, bights of coastline, etc, is a rather different business from berthing in a sheltered harbour. A great deal more consideration must be paid to present and expected weather conditions, tidal streams, passing commercial traffic, swinging room, and so on.

Shelter from Waves

The two most important considerations are wind and waves, both of which can cause considerable discomfort and danger to an anchored vessel. Generally, these two go hand in hand, but not always. The presence and the behaviour of a swell outside the anchorage must be considered with care, as long swells tend to curve round corners, much like long wavelength radio waves. Short waves, such as those directly generated by the wind, will not go round corners, so an anchorage sheltered from the wind will also be protected from these waves. Long swells, left over from a previous or distant wind, will often, however, bend round into the most apparently sheltered anchorage and make it quite untenable.

Shelter from Wind

High ground around the anchorage may seem to provide the best shelter, but this is not always so. The presence of valleys between surrounding hills may funnel an offshore wind down into an anchorage and accelerate it to alarming proportions (see the section on katabatic winds in chapter 7). Scottish lochs are prone to this, and the violence of these squalls can drag even the most firmly embedded ground tackle, as well as make life onboard somewhat uncomfortable. Low ground, on the other hand, may provide excellent shelter from waves, but none whatever from the wind. The best shelter is usually provided by moderately high ground covered in trees, which break and filter the wind thus preventing squalls, back eddies, and so on. Generally, waves cause the most discomfort and potential danger to an anchored boat, due to the

Photo 18 *Rivers such as the Ore in Suffolk that have very fast tidal streams can be dangerous places in any strength of wind against the stream for dinghy payloads like this.*

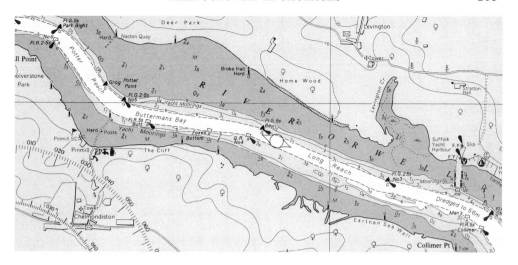

movement and snubbing on the cable, so the main criterion must be shelter from these.

Fig 73 This reach is about three miles long. At spring tides, conditions can become very rough in nor'west and south-east gales.

Tidal Streams in an Anchorage

Strong tidal streams can also render an apparently sheltered anchorage most uncomfortable, caused by the steep waves that can be kicked up when they run against the wind. Ebb tides in rivers, reinforced by the outgoing river water, can often be serious culprits here, especially if a big swell is rolling in over an entry bar. This swell, as mentioned earlier, can roll round a number of corners before attenuating, and with a fierce ebb against it will often produce extremely uncomfortable and dangerous conditions inside an apparently sheltered river. The further up the river you can get, and the more corners you can place between you and the bar, the more comfortable you will be. Bear in mind, however, that in some parts of a river there may be quite a long fetch for the wind, and, if it blows against the ebb, short, very steep seas can be kicked up, causing a light vessel, especially if anchored on rope, to

range around her cable quite violently (see figure 73). They can also make getting ashore by dinghy, and back aboard again, distinctly hazardous. This must be a serious consideration when picking an anchorage where you wish to go ashore.

The very speed of a tidal stream can also cause extra strains on ground tackle and make rowing ashore by dinghy almost impossible in certain places around half-tide.

The Holding Ground

The nature of the holding ground must also be considered when selecting an anchorage, some types of bottom being more effective than others. Small anchors printed on the chart often indicate the best holding, but these are usually for the benefit of large vessels and generally you will be able to find good anchorage in a more sheltered spot or closer to the shore. Sand, thick mud and clay provide the best holding for an

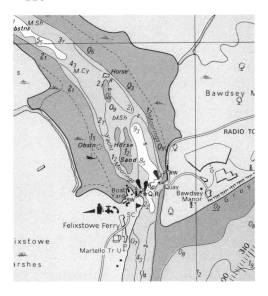

Fig 74 *There are many restrictions on anchoring in this entrance: underwater cable and ferry at the entrance, yacht moorings just inside, and the drying patches at Horse Sand and near the Horse buoy. Close to the entrance the tide runs very fast as it accelerates to get through the narrow gap. Further up, the deep channel is very narrow and it would be dangerous to anchor here if there was commercial traffic using the river.*

anchor, and rock, weed, fine sand or thin mud the worst. The type of bottom will be marked on the chart amongst the soundings. Underwater power cables provide excellent holding – but can be expensive to replace if you sever them. Keep well clear of them (marked by beacons on the shore) and also other anchor cables, mooring chains, etc (see figure 74).

You should use a tripping line if there is a likelihood of picking up a chain, or if you anchor in rock in which the anchor flukes can jam. Rock and weed, however, should be avoided if at all possible, as they make very poor holding ground, especially for modern anchors. The traditional fisherman's anchor holds best in these bottoms, but should be rigged with a tripping line since the flukes can easily wedge solidly under rocks. It is a simple matter to check the nature of the bottom before anchoring, by taking a sounding with the lead 'armed'.

Commercial Traffic

Passing commercial traffic in a river must also be taken into account when selecting an anchorage. These days many small rivers play host to ships so big that they cannot afford to move more than a few feet from their selected track down the main channel. It is absolutely imperative that you ensure that there is not the slightest chance of your boat swinging round into this channel under any circumstances. The damage such ships will do by ploughing steadily through the middle of your saloon is likely to be considerably less than that caused by them attempting to avoid you, especially in conditions of strong tides or winds. You may draw your own conclusions about the action the skipper or pilot might take in the middle of a wild night when confronted by your riding light in the middle of the channel, and hundreds of other boats moored close along the edges.

Even if you are anchored or moored well clear of the channel, these ships can make life uncomfortable by the wash they create. If you are in an alongside berth this wash can be enough to cause warps to part and all sorts of damage to be inflicted on your boat. A drying berth can be quite dangerous in such conditions if you are almost aground. It is not so much excessive speed as such, as the effect that shallow water on the edge of the channel has on the waves created by his passing (see chapter 7). Very large vessels in narrow channels can even generate what is known as 'canal effect', drawing the water away from the shallows as they approach, then letting it pour back again after passing (see figure 75). This can have serious consequences for a boat that is only just afloat, as you can imagine.

Swinging Circle

When calculating depths in the anchorage, make sure there will be sufficient depth at Low Water throughout your projected stay. If the tides are making up to springs, you may find the depth at Low Water decreases quite noticeably over a couple of days. Also ensure that sufficient depth is maintained throughout all the area of your swinging circle, and leave a good safety margin to allow for meteorological effects on the tide; and also for the possibility of canal effect from a passing coaster if you are anchored in a narrow commercial riv-

Fig 75 *Bow and stern waves are forced by the close banks of a narrow channel to push out ahead and astern of the vessel, creating a deep trough amidships. This can cause water to be suddenly sucked off the surrounding shallows as the vessel passes.*

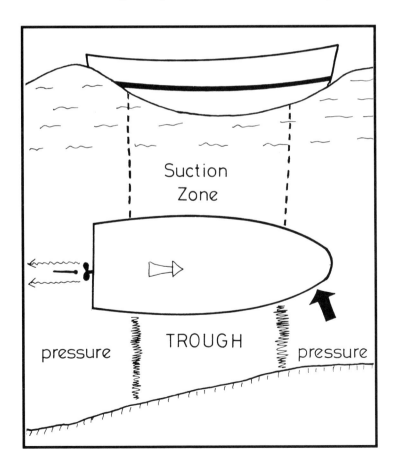

Suction Zone

TROUGH

pressure   pressure

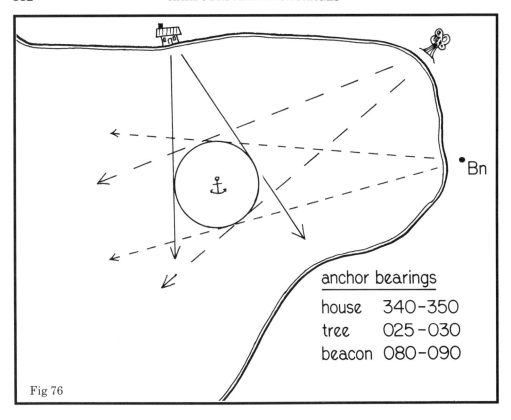

anchor bearings

house	340–350
tree	025–030
beacon	080–090

Fig 76

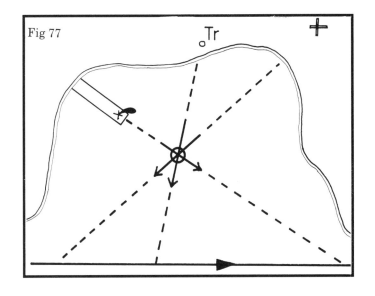

Fig 77

er. Your maximum swinging circle will have a radius of approximately your boat's length plus the amount of anchor warp out.

Anchor Bearings

Having anchored safely, you must then ensure that you stay there. From the navigational standpoint this means taking anchor bearings so that you have, in effect, a fix of your anchored position and can thus tell if you drag. You will, of course, swing round the anchor as the tide and wind change, so your position will be a circle rather than a point. The anchor bearings should consist of three clearing bearings to mark the edges of the swinging circle rather than an actual fix (see figure 76).

Shooting up an Anchorage

This is a useful trick for finding the precise position of a boat already in an anchorage, if you have such a large vessel that you want to check for swinging space before proceeding in. What you do is pass slowly across the entrance to the anchorage and shoot the compass bearings of a series of three (if possible) transits between the anchored vessel and objects ashore. If the reciprocals of these bearings are then plotted on the chart seawards from the shore objects they will intersect at the anchored vessel's position (see figure 77). This technique can also be used to fix any object whose position you are uncertain of, such as navigation buoys (see chapter 6).

Bear in mind, however, that that is the vessel's position and not necessarily that of her anchor. You may be able to estimate the anchor position from observing how the cable grows and by considering the current state of tide and wind. Otherwise call the vessel on VHF and ask.

10
Piloting in Fog

This is known as blind pilotage, and in certain respects it is a great deal more demanding than navigating offshore in the same conditions, as there are more things to bang into. On the other hand there is considerably more information available to assist you in finding and keeping track of your position, and it is surprising what an experienced and competent pilot can achieve in conditions of zero visibility. A good blind passage through coastal waters is an intensely satisfying achievement.

Nevertheless, the satisfaction of such potential achievement must not tempt the prudent skipper into using poor visibility as a playground. However experienced and capable he may be, however many reliable electronic aids he may have on board, fog remains the most dangerous of all conditions to be met with at sea. It should be treated with the utmost caution at all times (see chapter 7).

Electronic navigation aids, such as Decca, RDF, radar, etc, clearly make position-finding in fog a great deal easier, but it is vital that they are at all times considered as *aids* and no more. All have their limitations in terms of accuracy and reliability, which we will look at in detail later in this chapter

and in chapter 14; and in small boats you cannot always be certain of getting electricity into them. A wise skipper will always run a proper DR plot in conjunction, and will also at all times maintain a simple plan for getting out of trouble should the electronics fail.

Log, Lead and Lookout

These are the three traditional, simple and reliable tools for piloting in fog, along with compass and chart. The leadline, usually backing up an echosounder, is perhaps the most useful of all. It is totally reliable, unaffected by the extent of visibility, the effects of leeway, tidal stream or helmsman's error, and it gives you absolute information as opposed to an estimated position. If it tells you that you are in three metres of water with a sandy bottom, then it matters not whether you are in Tarbert or Timaru, weather and tidal height permitting, you can safely anchor and wait for the fog to lift, knowing for certain that you are at least well clear of the passage of large shipping.

With a traditional leadline, hollowed out at the bottom for 'arming' with tallow or lard, you can take a sounding and also bring up a sample of the seabed.

Knowing whether you are over sand or mud or shells or whatever can sometimes be of great help in ascertaining your position. This trick was employed regularly and to great effect by seamen in the old days, who with experience in one particular area could often define their positions with considerable accuracy from a seabed sample.

The use of the log was discussed in detail in chapters 2 and 5; and the echo-sounder in chapters 2, 6 and 8.

Keeping the Lookout

Keeping a lookout should also include a listening watch, as much often can be learnt this way. Send a man for'ard and maintain strict silence on the boat so that he stands the maximum chance

Photo 19 *Land disappears into the murk as fog falls on the coast. There should be a good fix on the chart by now, and the skipper will have posted lookouts and settled down to the often tense business of blind pilotage.*

of hearing surf, shore traffic noises, bell-buoys, foghorns and the like. If under power, stop the engine now and again and listen carefully for a minute or two in the silence. If you hear a foghorn, reply with the correct signal from your own (see appendix 2). It may be worth listening with your ear against the hull below water now and again, as propeller noises carry a long way underwater. It will be almost impossible to gauge the direction of a noise, but at least it will alert you to the presence of a power vessel. With experience you may be able to assess a very rough range and the type of ship (small or large, basically).

Visual lookout in fog can be very tiring and the constant writhing of the fog seems to create solid shapes where none exist. Spells of looking out should be restricted to about half an hour at a time if sufficient crew are available to alternate. Clearest visibility seems to be at sea level (where white bow-waves, surf, etc, can be seen) and also from the corner of the eye (see chapter 3).

Radiation fog may be very low-lying and it can often be helpful to have a lookout up the mast in such conditions, where he may see the masts of other vessels, tall lighthouses and so on (see next section).

The Type of Fog

If the fog is known to be the radiation type that flows off the land at night, the skipper should know that it will almost certainly clear up during the morning, so he needs only to keep his vessel safe and in a position from which he knows

for certain the direction of his destination, until the fog clears (see chapter 7). He can anchor close in (dangers permitting), follow a contour line slowly towards the haven, or even stand offshore out of the fog until it does lift.

However, in sea fog things are very different and it may be necessary to make for a temporary haven that is easily entered in poor visibility while waiting for it to clear. Because sound propagation in fog is unreliable it is most unwise to rely on a pierhead fog signal to guide you into harbour. It is equally unwise to depend on fog signals from lighthouses or buoys in order to venture into dangerous inshore waters (see later section).

Following Depth Contours

Suitable depth contours can be followed very efficiently and safely by means of an echo-sounder, and this is perhaps one of the safest ways to pilot in poor visibility. For reasonable accuracy the contour should be fairly smooth and on a steeply shelving bottom so that it is

Fig 78

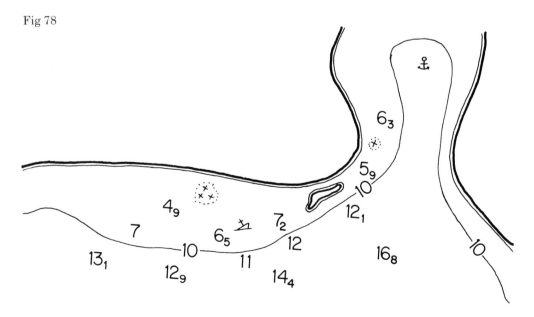

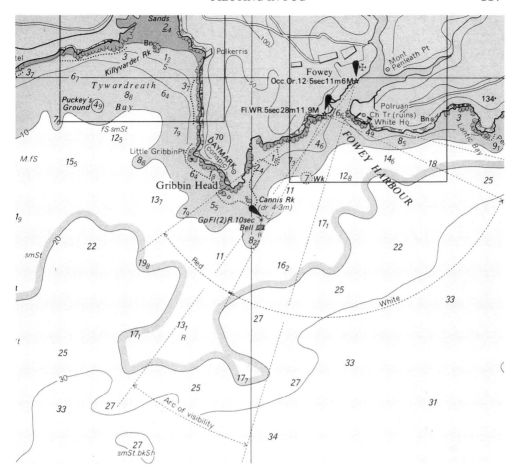

Fig 79

clearly delineated. One such as shown in figure 78 is ideal for the purpose and can be followed right round the headland and into the bay or river, where you can then anchor clear of shipping and other dangers. Even if the contour does not go right into a river it may very well pass close enough to a harbour entrance for you to pick up visually a breakwater or lighthouse (see also later sections on landfall techniques). Contours on gradually shelving bottoms cover too wide an area to be followed safely, and those that meander a lot can cause much confusion as it is easy to lose track of which side of a loop you are on (see figure 79).

The best way to follow a contour is to zig-zag inshore and offshore across it, making a small alteration when you head in (so as to almost parallel the contour) and a fairly large one – perhaps 30° or so – when you head out, so as to avoid the risk of running too shallow during the turn. However, if the contour is deep, and no dangers lie close inshore of it, better progress can be made with small alterations both in and out. Watch out, though, for bends in the contour which may necessitate larger alterations to regain the depth without too much delay (see figure 80 and chapter 11).

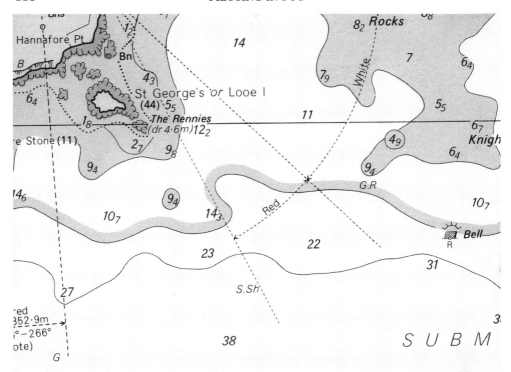

Fig 80

Line of Soundings

Another way of using the sounder (or leadline) if suitable contours are not available to follow is to 'run a line of soundings'. This technique consists of taking a series of soundings and simultaneous log and time readings while running along a set course. Then take a piece of paper and plot the depths along the edge, their distances apart being to the scale of the chart. You can then juggle this paper around the chart in the vicinity of your EP at the start of the run until the series of soundings line up reasonably well with a series on the chart (see figure 81). This will give you a very useful, if approximate, check on your DR track. If you have tracing paper you will find it easier to use, as you can then see all the depths beneath it on the chart as you move it around.

Buoy Hopping

Although strictly speaking one should not rely on buoys for fixing position, following a line of them may well be the least of a number of evils when entering a river or harbour in fog. Some care needs to be taken to ensure that the disposition of the buoys is such that you can be virtually certain of finding the next one each time. If this is not the case, then the method may well get you into a worse position than you were in to begin with. The buoys should also be either numbered or named, so that

Fig 82 It should be apparent that mistaking the first port-hand buoy for the second could easily lead to disaster. This exercise is safest with a weak foul stream running directly along the channel.

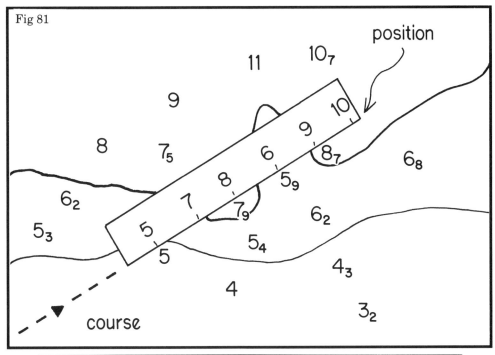

Fig 81

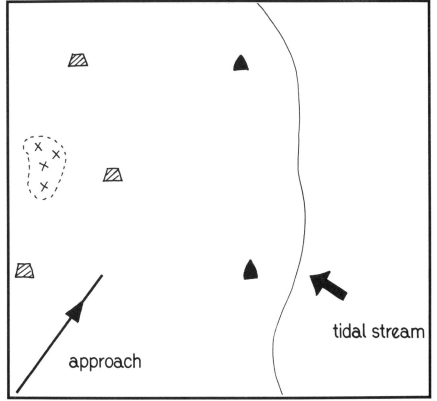

each can be positively identified then crossed off on the chart or in the navigator's notebook as you pass it. With unmarked buoys dotted about unevenly and a strong tidal stream you could end up quite lost (see figure 82).

Echo-ranging

Echo-ranging can sometimes be used to determine a distance off steep cliffs. If you sound a short blast on your horn and then time how long it takes for the echo to return, you can then calculate from the speed of sound (approximately 1,100ft/335m per second) how far you are off the cliff. Remember that the sound travels there and back, so the total travelling time must be halved in order to find the one-way distance that you want. Thus, halve the time taken for the echo to return, then multiply this by 1,100 to get the range in feet (or by 335 to get the range in metres). Then divide by three to get yards. Or, if you prefer, multiply total echo time (there and back) by 183 to get yards off. A nautical mile, by way of a reminder, is 6,000 feet long (2,000 yards).

Ancillary Guides to Position

There are many other (at times) useful guides to your rough position, particularly when very close inshore. Church bells, traffic, dogs barking, surf roaring, seagulls squawking, etc, can all help generally to orientate you when feeling your way along a coastline in fog. Check carefully on the chart as to from where along the coast a particular noise might be coming – church bells, for example, are likely to be emanating from a church; heavy concentrations of squawking seagulls may indicate the proximity of a fishing harbour (or a garbage dump!) and so on. Even smells

can at times be of assistance, those of fish and chips carrying a long way out to sea in light offshore breezes.

Changing wave patterns can also indicate the presence of banks or headlands to windward, steep cliffs or harbour walls to leeward. In the first instance the seas will become calmer as you get in the lee, even of shallow submerged banks. In the second, the seas are likely to become confused because of the backwash from the cliff or harbour wall (see chapter 7).

Making Landfall

This is perhaps the most nerve-racking part of navigating in fog. When a boat is close to the coast the skipper usually has sufficient idea of his position to creep at least into the shallows and anchor, if only while he sorts himself out. Standing in from seaward, though, is a very different matter, and the basic aim of the prudent pilot should be not to arrive at his destination as such, but to arrive at a safe part of the coast that is clear of dangers and blessed with usable depth contours. This should be combined with the offset landfall principle (see chapter 3) so that on arrival he knows for certain which way a safe haven lies, if not actually his destination.

Landfall on a Depth Contour

Many places will be found to have depth contours and other guides, such as bell-buoys, etc, that will enable you to make a similar type of landfall. A suitable contour line that simply follows round into a bay or harbour where safe anchorage can be found is as good as anything, but it will require you to make an offset landfall (see chapter 3) in order to be certain on which side of the entrance you are when you reach the contour.

Clearly, the best side of an entrance on which to make your landfall is that with the steepest and straightest depth contour that is well clear of dangers. If both sides are similar, then you may well be pressured into one or the other by such factors as wind direction and tidal stream. You should make for the side that needs the least accurate course from offshore. If one side requires you to tack and the other needs only a straightforward reach, then clearly the reaching one should enable the most accurate course to be plotted into it. If the wind is not a deciding factor, then you should generally aim to land up down-tide of the entrance, so that you have a slow and controlled approach along the depth contour, stemming the tide. The most important thing is to be absolutely certain on arrival which side you are.

The Position Circle Principle

This was discussed in chapter 6. I used the technique once to good effect when I got into a spot of navigational bother off Lyme Bay in thick fog, when the compass had been fitted the wrong way round. Pessimistic estimates of errors produced a positional circle about 10 miles in diameter. Fortunately, Lyme Bay is blessed with some very useful depth contours, and we managed to reduce this circle to a spot fix by the simple expedient of steering the vessel into the middle of the bay until we hit the 20 fathom line (this was before the days of metric charts). This immediately turned the position circle into a roughly east-west position line some 10 miles long, which we steered to the west until we hit the 10 fathom line that runs more or less due south down the western end of the bay. Crossing the line with the contour produced a reasonable two-

point fix. This contour also happened to pass about 50 yards outside a large isolated rock called the Ore Stone, so we just followed it slowly and carefully until the rock appeared out of the fog. An idea of the accuracy of this can be gauged from the fact that we sighted the rock two minutes before I estimated we would (see figure 83).

Checking Visibility and Tidal Stream

The knowledge of the precise visibility and the precise tidal stream are invaluable to a navigator in fog. The first can be checked quite simply by throwing something over the side (bio-degradable for preference) and watching it out of sight. Time it or check the log reading before and after for accurate measurements if the visibility is not too poor. Bear in mind, however, that fog tends to fall and lift and generally vary the visibility frequently, so keep repeating this.

A tidal stream's strength and direction can be gauged with considerable accuracy by stemming it next to a buoy and checking compass and speedometer log (see chapter 8). If you cannot find a convenient buoy it may be worth anchoring if the water is not too deep and doing the same, although you will need to allow for any strength of wind affecting the way you lie. Watch how the water flows past the cable if you think the wind may be affecting the way you lie.

Fog Signals

Buoys, lighthouses, light vessels, harbour entrances, and so on, produce a variety of sound signals to assist the seaman in fog, and the type of signal

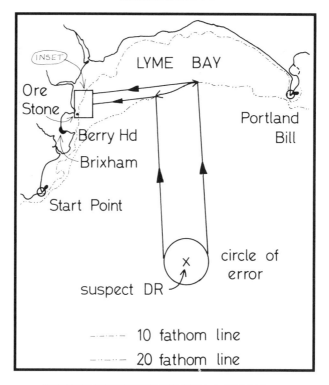

Fig 83

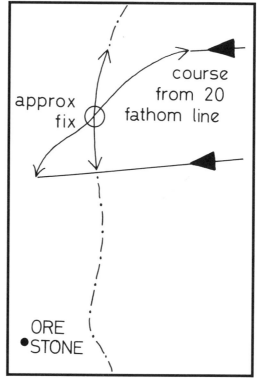

will be indicated on the chart. There are six main types of fog signal and they all produce different sounds.

Horn: sounds like a very loud car horn.

Reed: produces a high-pitched, rather weak sound.

Diaphone: makes a powerful low-pitched sound which generally ends with a distinctive grunt.

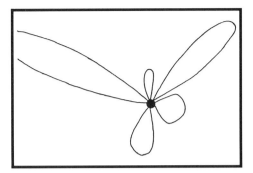

Fig 84

Siren: produces a variety of sounds but generally like a high-pitched wail.

Explosive: as implied, this sounds like the report from a gun.

Bells, Gongs and Whistles: these tend to be found on buoys and pierheads and the sounds do not carry very far. They are usually actuated by either machinery or wave motion. Care must be taken in very calm weather as the wave-operated type may be unreliable.

The ranges at which these various signals can be heard are extremely erratic and unreliable, because of the peculiarities of sound propagation in fog. The sound tends to travel in lobes of varying size and length (see figure 84), so that it can often disappear and reappear as a boat sails from one lobe to another, although remaining at a constant distance from the sound source. The sound can cease as a boat gets closer to the source if in doing so she moves out of a lobe. So the greatest caution must be exercised when utilising fog signals for navigation, and it must never be assumed that one will be heard as it is approached. Bear in mind also that in conditions of localised fog banks the signal may be in a clear area and so is not being sounded.

Using Radar

Radar, of course, is an extremely useful aid to blind pilotage, but it is most important that you understand how it works, how to tune the set properly, and the limitations and inherent inaccuracies of your particular set. Full details on tuning your set and adjusting clutter controls to give a clear picture without cutting out important echoes should be in the user's manual, and they should be studied most carefully.

However, what is unlikely to be mentioned in the manual are the limitations and inaccuracies of the set. So far as navigation is concerned there are three basic and very important factors that must be considered. The first is the fact that the radar signal is reflected more efficiently by some surfaces than by others; the second is the fact that the screen shows relative motion, not true; and the third is the effect on echoes of the horizontal width of the beam. These technical aspects of radar are dealt with in chapter 14.

Interpreting what is shown on the screen is also far from easy, and a specialist course in the operation of radar is strongly recommended if you have this tool on board.

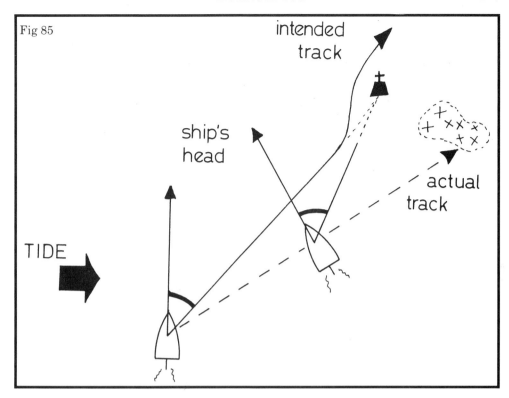

Fig 85

Collision Avoidance

The fact that the radar screen shows the movement of objects relative to your heading (up the screen) must be kept in mind at all times when using it to avoid colliding with ships, buoys, lighthouses, etc. A constant check must be maintained on the compass heading so as to avoid the danger, shown in figure 85, of circling round while trying to maintain a set bearing or distance from a navigational object. It is safest to take a sequence of relative bearings and distances from the screen, convert the bearings to Magnetic or True (according to your heading), then plot the

Photo 20 *A small yacht radar like this is not really suitable for accurate collision avoidance work, but it can be of great assistance when navigating in fog if it is used with care and an understanding of its limitations.*

sequence on the chart. The true picture of your changing relationship with the object will then be clear from the line of fixes – but see chapters 6 and 14 with reference to radar bearings.

A quick way to check whether an object – be it ship, buoy or lighthouse – is on a collision course is simply to place the bearing cursor over it and watch its progress while you maintain a steady course. If it travels along the cursor directly towards you (the centre of the screen), then the two of you will collide. If it moves up the screen ahead of the cursor it will pass ahead of you, and if it moves down below it will pass astern. This is exactly the same principle as a visual relative bearing. It is not, however, nearly so accurate and it will give no indication of the heading of a vessel nor the angle of view of a landmark. Neither will it give the immediate indi-

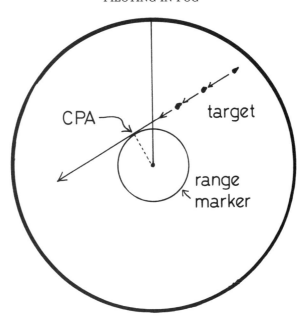

Fig 86 *While holding a steady course and speed you should plot on the screen at frequent intervals the position of the ship or object. When three or four plots have been made the positions can be joined up and extended across the screen in the direction of the movement. A line plotted from your position (centre of screen) to meet this line at right angles indicates (where it meets the line) the position of closest approach of the other vessel or object. The range of this can be checked with the range rings or variable range marker.*

cation of a sudden alteration of course by the other vessel, nor a sudden increase in tidal drift that a visual watch will.

A more accurate method is to plot a CPA ('closest point of approach') on the screen. The technique, whether used for avoiding ships or stationary objects in the presence of tidal stream or leeway, can be seen in figure 86. This is big ship stuff really, requiring large screens and very accurate radar pictures. Small yacht radars must be used in this manner with extreme caution, and only after considerable experience.

Cross-index Ranges

A useful technique that can be employed in suitable conditions is that of the cross-index range. The required range at which you wish to pass along a suitable coastline can be marked on the face of the radar screen as a line parallel to your heading marker. The boat is then simply steered so as to keep the coastline outside this line. The range can be set up using range rings or the variable range marker, and the line drawn with chinagraph pencil or similar. Great care must be taken with this technique to ensure that you identify correctly the actual part of the coast that is painting on the screen. This, as explained in chapter 14, may not be the clear line that is marked on the chart.

This same technique can also be used to pass a certain distance from an offshore danger, such as a lighthouse or lightship, but great care must be taken in this situation to make allowance for any cross stream that may be setting you onto the danger. It is important to

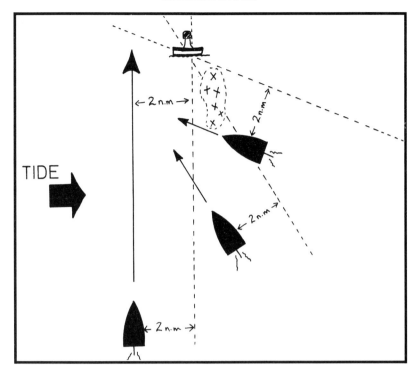

Fig 87 *This is what can happen to the skipper who peers at his screen and steers to keep on the cross-index line, without checking his heading and the actual bearing of the object. Shaping to pass two miles clear of the object he may be, but keeping in safe water he most certainly is not.*

appreciate that the picture you see on the screen is a relative one, not a true one. The cross-index range shown on the screen is the distance from your beam, not a plotted direction and distance on the chart. Figure 87 should make this clear (see also previous section and figure 85).

Generally it is better simply to use radar ranges as position lines and plot normal fixes on the chart than it is to attempt navigating directly on a small radar screen. Nevertheless, these techniques can be useful for entering harbours, etc, when time does not permit chart plotting. As mentioned earlier, it is essential that you appreciate the skill and experience required for safe navigation on a radar screen; you cannot simply read specific information off it as you can from a Decca Navigator, for instance.

Other Radio Aids

Many other radio aids to navigation can be used with varying degrees of reliability and accuracy for navigation in fog and they are discussed in detail in chapter 14.

11
Piloting Without Charts

This is not an exercise I would recommend, but there may come a time when for some urgent reason you need to enter a harbour for which you have no chart. You may also, in suitable conditions, simply wish to explore a creek or bay for which you have no detailed chart. This operation does not have to be foolhardy, if done properly and with certain precautions taken.

Several circumstances could cause you to need to enter a harbour without suitable charts, and it will be instructive to consider them. The most likely are when stress of weather, gear failure, loss of vital stores (water, diesel, etc), or medical problems force you to seek immediate shelter or shore assistance.

In theory you should carry a chart portfolio to cover all such likely eventualities, but in practice there is always the chance of perhaps being carried by bad weather or trouble beyond the area for which you are properly equipped.

Even if you do carry all the necessary charts there is also the risk of more prosaic problems such as the requisite one blowing over the side, or the watchkeeper tipping his cocoa over

the important bit of it. These apparently silly things do happen, and a sensible skipper must prepare himself mentally for the possibility. I once knew a very experienced professional skipper who made regular cross-Channel passages with a dogleg in the middle in order to circumvent a cocoa stain, under which lay he knew not what!

The financial cost of equipping your chart locker with large scale charts for all conceivable possibilities is clearly beyond the pockets of most normal sailors. Pilot Books, however, cover large areas, and it is relatively economical to ensure that sufficient Pilots are on board to cover anywhere you might possibly have to run to. A good Pilot should contain virtually all the information that is on the large scale chart, and a great deal – particularly about tidal streams, entry transits, etc – that is not. With care, a perfectly adequate chart can be constructed from the details in the Pilot Book, and the two, used in conjunction with certain common sense precautions that will be discussed, should enable a competent skipper to make a sound job of entering almost any haven in all but the most difficult of conditions.

Draw Your Own Chart

This is the first thing to do, and if you have a good Pilot Book of the area it is not as difficult as it sounds. The best type for this is an Admiralty Pilot, because of the wealth of accurate detail it contains. On the other hand, many yachtsmen's Pilots have chartlets of small harbours and creeks for which you may not possess charts, and these, with care, can often be used in themselves for navigating under suitable conditions, in conjunction with the written information.

The first part of the operation is much the same as was described in chapter 9, where initial preparations for entering harbour were discussed. In this instance, however, you will not have the large scale entry chart to peruse, so you must study as carefully as possible the largest scale chart you do have that contains the harbour. The mass of information in the Pilot Book should enable the sketchy picture on the chart to gradually become much more detailed in your mind.

Not until you have this good, clear mental image of the harbour should you begin to draw it. Put a large piece of paper on the chart table and draw on it a square or rectangle big enough to encompass the harbour. Knowing from the Pilot and the small scale chart the size of the harbour, you can calculate the scale to draw it to and insert this as a ruler line, together with an arrow

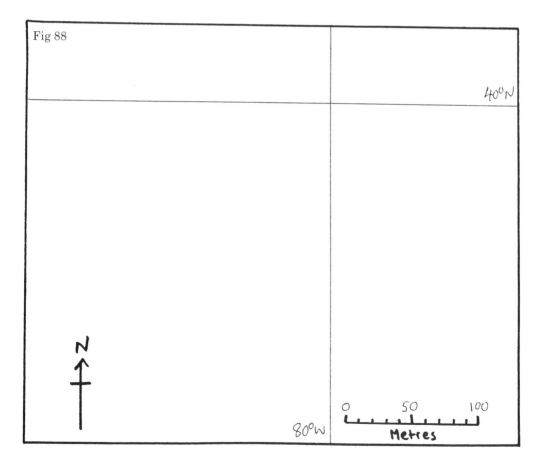

Fig 88

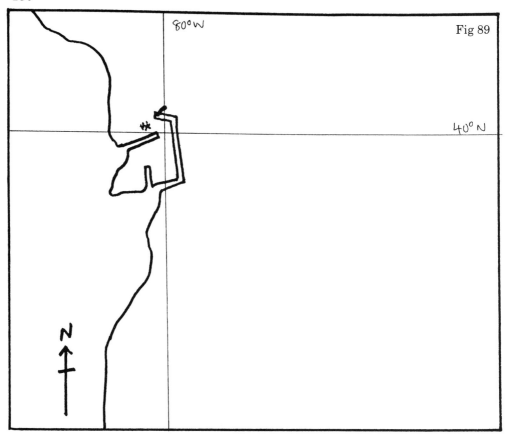

80°W

Fig 89

40°N

N

pointing north. Put them where your mental picture shows they will not obscure detail. If you cannot do this then your image of the harbour is not good enough and you must continue studying it until it is. Then plot latitude and longitude lines for a distinctive feature of the harbour, and you will have a basic structure for your chart (see figure 88).

Now you can gradually flesh out this skeleton with details from the Pilot. Imagine that the harbour is something like the one in figure 89. This, or even less, might be all the detail shown on the small scale chart, but it should be sufficient to construct the basic outline of the harbour. Begin by plotting the feature for which you have inserted the latitude and longitude. Then measure from the

small scale chart the ranges and bearings from this object of other salient features – buoys, beacons, lights, rocks, ends and corners of jetties, prominent buildings, and so on – and carefully plot these on your chart. Relevant positions can then be joined up to create an outline of banks, jetties, etc, to give a good basic chart (see figure 90).

The remaining information in the Pilot – moorings, buoys, depths, drying patches and suchlike – can then be added to this outline in order to produce a competent and fairly accurate chart such as can be seen in figure 91. With the help of the Pilot Book and some seamanlike common sense, this chart should be perfectly adequate for entering the harbour. On finishing

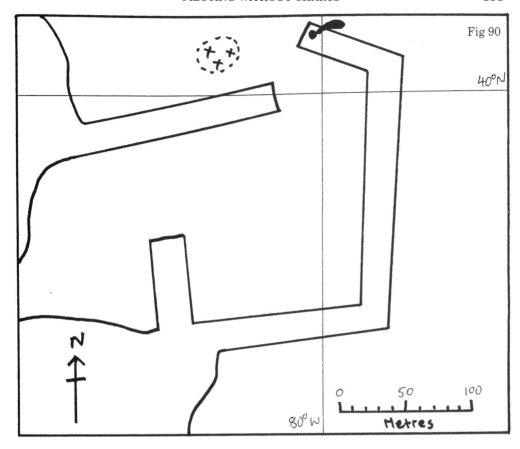

Fig 90

40°N

0   50   100

80° W

Metres

it you should then cross-check all the information very carefully against the Pilot and the small scale chart before finally accepting it as a working chart.

Making Pilotage Notes

This was discussed both in chapter 2 and chapter 9, but it will do no harm to reiterate its usefulness and importance, particularly in these circumstances. Clearly, more details must be noted in the navigator's notebook as in this situation you do not have a detailed, professional chart to check and peruse. Much of the more important information contained in the Pilot could usefully be paraphrased and noted down for quick reference.

Seamanlike Precautions

However good your chart seems to be, you should still take certain precautions to protect yourself against inaccuracies. The first thing to do is heave to just off the entrance on arrival and take a long and careful look at the harbour to see how it compares with your chart. Check the angles of jetties, the positions of lights and buoys, prominent buildings, and so on. Bear in mind the angle from which you are viewing the entrance and try to visualise from the chart how things should look from this angle and from a horizontal viewpoint. As discussed earlier in the book, this business of translating the vertical view of a chart into the horizontal view of the

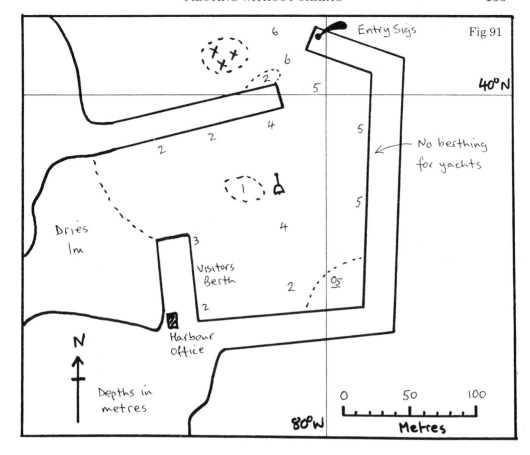

eye is not always easy, and it is perhaps even less so with a home-made chart plotted in pencil, without the colours and distinguishing shading that helps the eye on a professional chart.

If you have VHF radio and the harbour has a Port Operations Frequency you can call them, explain your situation and ask advice on entering and berthing. This is particularly useful when entering a large commercial port as they will furnish you with details of big ship movements and the general activity in the harbour and its approach-

es. They may even have a wandering launch that could guide you in.

Look out for navigational buoys and beacons for guidance, but bear in mind that beacons right by the bank may not be indicative of deep water except when the tide is up. Occasionally you may find tide gauges on inshore beacons, showing the depth of water at the beacon, so look out for these.

Using the Tide

If there are shallow or drying patches inside or near the entrance then try to enter on the flood tide, so that you will lift off again easily should you run aground. If half-tide drying patches exist, then enter early on the flood if

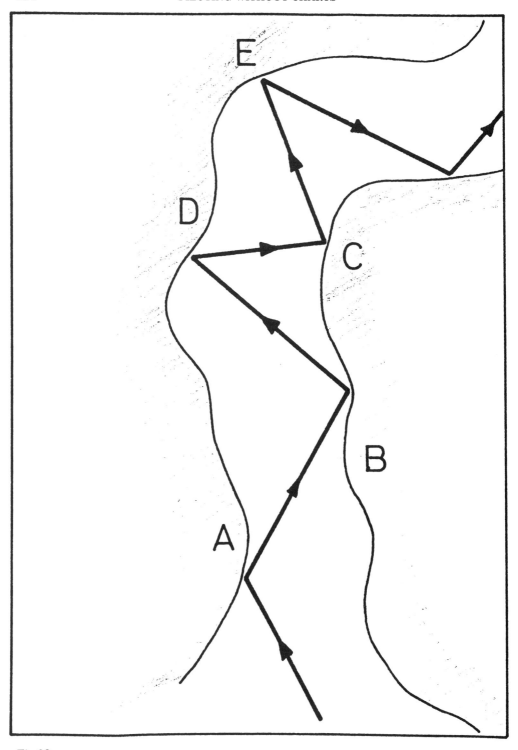

Fig 92

you can, while they are still uncovered and you can thus see them.

Long, narrow harbours with strong streams are often better entered against the ebb, as you will travel more slowly over the ground with greater control over the boat and thus have more time to observe the features, sort out your course and keep clear of other shipping. If the ebb is very strong – as it often is if the harbour is at the entrance to a river (due to the tidal stream being reinforced by river water running seaward) – then aim to enter during the last of the ebb when it is not too strong. In certain harbours this stage of the tide may expose the deep channels clearly and make the pilotage much easier anyway. All these techniques, and more, have already been discussed in earlier chapters, but this is the occasion on which they become particularly important.

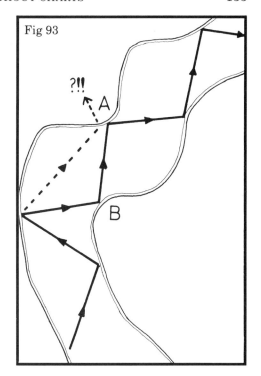

Fig 93

Piloting Uncharted Creeks

This is a slightly different game as there will likely be no information available to you. Nevertheless, in suitable conditions and with a suitable boat it can be a perfectly feasible and extremely interesting exercise.

Once again, much of the information in earlier chapters will be especially useful here, particularly chapters 7 and 8. With that knowledge you will probably find that the general lie of a main channel in narrow creeks can often be assessed with surprising accuracy.

Make your entry as early as possible on the flood, when the channel will be most clearly delineated, and errors easily corrected (running aground). A zig-zag technique as shown in figure 92 is an excellent fail-safe method of negotiating winding channels when the tide has covered the edges of the deep water. Make each alteration of course, on run-

ning shallow, sufficiently bold that you are certain the next leg will take you to the other side.

Keep track of your progress if the creek is charted but simply unmarked, so that you know roughly when you are approaching a very sharp bend such as that in figure 93. As you can see in the diagram, you will need to make very bold alterations of course in order to be certain of crossing to the other bank while rounding such a bend.

Withys (thin branches stuck in the mud to mark the channel) will often be found in apparently unmarked creeks – usually put there by the locals to assist them in navigating. Sometimes they will carry simple, correctly-coloured topmarks, such as painted baked bean tins or old oil cans of suitable colour, so look out for the rusted remnants of these. Otherwise you will have to study carefully the general lie of the channel

Fig 94

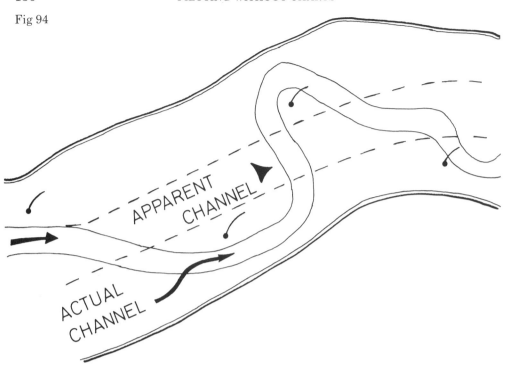

in order to ascertain on which side each withy lies. From a distance they can be very confusing.

When the creek becomes very narrow near its head you will usually find that the deep water meanders back and forth even when there is no apparent reason for it to do so. Withys that appear to mark a straight stretch will nearly always actually be on opposing sides of a winding channel, as you can see in figure 94. They will also very often be stuck in the mud outside the edge of the channel, so do not assume that deep water lies close up to them.

Use of Leadline and Anchor

In conditions like these an echo-sounder, perhaps thirty feet abaft your stem, is likely to be of little use in warning of shallow water ahead. Far more

efficient is to have someone casting the lead continuously from right for'ard, and proceed slowly enough to stop if depths shoal too much. You can then cast around like a bloodhound to find the deep water before proceeding. Exploring such places is much easier under power than under sail as you can stop, back and fill as necessary.

If you are creeping up on the flood under sail it may be worth having a sheet anchor rigged aft which can be let go if you ground. This should hold you in line with the channel, pointing the way you want to go, as the tide rises and floats you off. You can then haul back into the deep water before weighing and proceeding. You will need to check the effect of wind strength and direction before doing this, but it is likely to be more effective than letting go the bower anchor and perhaps swinging all over the place before sufficient tide makes for you to sail clear.

Observing the Water

The famous voyagers of the Pacific Islands could interpret the varying shapes of waves caused by overlapping swells and wave-trains with sufficient accuracy to help them navigate thousands of miles across vast tracts of ocean. Years of experience and training were needed for this, but the modern coastal navigator can learn enough to help him greatly in his identification of channels, shallows and banks.

Lacking any influence other than a single wind direction acting on the sea, waves will assume a simple and regular sinusoidal shape. In reality, of course, even the steadiest of winds varies in strength and direction sufficiently to make the wave-train rather less regular than this. An underlying swell from a different direction – from a gale elsewhere perhaps, or left over from the previous wind – will add further confusion to this theoretical regular pattern.

These sorts of irregularities will give us very little in the way of useful navigational information. What is much more instructive is the alteration in wave shape and pattern caused by shallow water and strong tidal streams, as discussed in chapter 7. When sufficient contrast exists in nearby conditions the differences in wave patterns become distinct enough to give useful guidance to the navigator.

An extreme example of this may be found in certain gulfs in the islands off the West Coast of Scotland, where the main tidal stream flows very strongly close to a back eddy almost as strong. If one of these streams is running with the wind, the other will be against it and there will be a very clear line between the smooth water where wind and tide are together and the rough, steep waves in the area where they are opposed. Less extreme, but similar examples may be found almost anywhere where the tidal streams run at any strength. The waves in a main channel, where the stream runs strongest, often will be quite distinctly different from those in the surrounding shallows, especially when the sides of the channel are steep enough to give a clear delineation between deep and shallow water.

Even without the influence of a strong tidal stream the shallow water itself may well show shorter and steeper seas than those in the deep channel, with perhaps even a clear line of breakers along the edge of the bank. This is quite commonly experienced on the East Coast of England where relatively deep swatchways run through steep-sided banks. This can be a very useful guide to the edge of deep water as long as the delineation is not confused by wind-over-tide conditions in the main channel.

Colour of the Water

As a guide to position this can be useful in certain circumstances, but it needs to be treated with some caution. If you look at aerial photographs of estuaries and harbour approaches you can often see quite clearly the colour difference between deep and shallow water. Unfortunately it is far more difficult to spot this difference from the low viewpoint of a boat on the water, although in certain conditions of light and depth it can be done, the shallow water generally looking browner and muddier (over suitably muddy bottoms) than the deep.

In sunny conditions with variable cloud cover, especially cumulus, this sign must be treated with great caution, however, as brownish patches of water will appear in places where the clouds throw a shadow.

Tide-lines and Eddies

These are caused by tidal streams meeting, rather than by variations in the seabed, so are not directly useful for position checking. In certain situations, though, they can provide a useful guide in places where you know more or less where these streams should meet.

Eddies are often caused by submerged rocks, especially in places like the Channel Islands where very strong tides swirl about over rocky bottoms. Unfortunately they rarely surface directly over the rock they mark, so can only provide a very approximate indication at best of the rock's whereabouts.

Tide-lines are usually marked quite clearly by a line of froth and rubbish caught in the slack water between two tidal streams that are running into each other. If you know where these streams meet, then the tide-line can be a very useful guide to position, although this meeting place often moves about as the tide ebbs and floods. In tight places with strong tides, however, they often need to be crossed with some caution, as the opposing streams can twist the boat right round as the bow gets into one while the stern remains in the other. When I lived in the Channel Islands this was often employed by experienced local boatmen as a 'party piece' to impress visitors. They would roar straight towards a wall of rocks with apparently no intention of altering course to avoid them, then at the last moment cross the tide-line which would swing the boat sharp round and spit her straight through the clear gap!

The Lie of a Channel

Much help can be gained, when negotiating estuaries and rivers, from an understanding of the way a deep channel tends naturally to lie between its drying banks. Like most things, ourselves included, water always attempts to follow the path of least resistance. Thus we can often make a good educated guess at where it will tend to flow if we know the nature of the obstacles it is attempting to negotiate. This can tell us not only where the deep channel is likely to be, but also where the tidal stream will run strongest, which can be of great benefit when struggling up an estuary against the ebb with pub closing time fast approaching.

With no undue influences on its movement the water will simply flow up and down the middle of the creek or whatever, but the moment something gets in its way it will take the easy route. Perhaps the best known case of this is on bends in rivers or creeks, where the water will get halfway past the bend before encountering shallows and being made to turn. This invariably scours out the deepest channel on the outside of the bend. The water then overshoots the turn, tending to bring the channel back into the centre or even across to the other side (see chapter 4 for more information on the behaviour of streams).

The slope of the banks at half-tide can also indicate the position of best water if they vary noticeably, the deepest water usually being close to the steeper bank. And it is worth bearing in mind that buoys in small, drying creeks can be deceptively positioned at this stage of the tide, especially when they mark the outsides of bends. The stream running towards the outside will often lay the buoy across into the shallows outside the channel, and it is far from unknown

Photo 22 *A fairly typical spit of mud extending well out from the saltings at the intersection of two channels. Note that the withys do not mark the very end of this spit.*

to find these buoys dried out yards from the channel as Low Water approaches.

Forks in a channel need to be negotiated with some care near High Water, as invariably a long drying spit extends from the central bank, forcing the channels to divide some way before reaching the land that lies between them. These spits also tend to reach out from headlands lying on the insides of bends.

Moored Boats

Moorings in rivers are generally laid on either side of the main channel and with some care can often be used more or less as navigation buoys. However, common sense must be utilised along with the echo-sounder; moorings may dry or be in very shallow water (as may navigation buoys in small rivers and creeks). Consider the sizes and types of the boats on them and keep midway between the lines, where the centre of the channel will almost certainly lie. Beware the large yacht with a lifting keel that could delude you into expecting deep water! If you have no guides like these, then look for your deep water, and the indications of it, where it is most likely to be – on the outside of river bends, for example, or close by commercial ship wharves.

Surveying by Dinghy

If time and circumstances permit, you can very profitably lie at anchor just off the uncharted section and go in with the dinghy and leadline to sound out the channel. This can also be done before entering uncharted anchorages and small harbours, and it is a most valuable and little-used tool in the armoury of the pilot.

Great care must be taken, however, especially when surveying harbours or drying berths, to drag the leadline back and forth all over the approach and over the berth itself, to ensure that no lumps, large rocks, bedsteads, old cookers, etc, stick up from the satisfactory depths that the leadline shows. A berth alongside an old harbour wall should also be checked for protuberances below the surface, by dragging the leadline along the wall itself.

Drying berths require particular care, as was discussed in chapter 9, and you should be very wary of lying in an uncharted one unless you have inspected it closely at Low Water or unless it is used regularly by locals who tell you it is safe.

Taking a Pilot

Large ships do this all the time and there is no reason why, in certain situations, yachts and motor cruisers should not do the same. In areas such as the English East Coast, where harbours are often surrounded by drying sandbanks that frequently shift position after onshore gales, pilots are usually available for small craft, and details will generally be found in Pilot Books and Almanacs.

You should always bear in mind when taking a pilot aboard that you, the skipper, still retain the responsibility for the safety of the vessel. This can cause some tricky situations at times, and you should be extremely wary of taking on a 'pilot' who is not officially recognised by the Almanac or Pilot Book. We have all had experience of locals who 'know where the best water is' or who tell us 'there is plenty of water there for you'. Experienced fishermen usually can be relied upon to know the local waters as they negotiate them virtually every day of their lives in all conditions of wind and stream and darkness.

12
Coastal Shipping

The presence of shipping, perhaps in large numbers, in relatively restricted spaces at times can present great difficulties and dangers to the inshore navigator. Partly this is because of the risk of collision and partly at times because of the difficulty of keeping an accurate positional plot when constantly having to alter course and speed to avoid other shipping. For a small boat the simplest solution to both these problems is to alter course clear of any vessel on a steady bearing, in sufficient time that the alteration can be very slight. This both ensures comfortable avoidance of collision and simple, minimal alteration to the plot. Note time, log reading and new course in the logbook, and again when resuming the proper course. You can then make the necessary correction to your DR plot. Keeping well clear of shipping in busy waters will also avoid the frequently occurring problem of a ship close to you making a sudden, apparently incomprehensible, alteration of course to avoid another ship that he can see but you cannot. This can have serious effects both on your nerves and your DR plot.

A frightening number of ships appear to steam around close inshore with no-one on watch, and even those that do keep watch, and have seen you, and intend giving way to you (if required to do so), will not alter course until the very last moment. They may have calculated, with their computers and their full-size chart tables, their accurate courses and speeds, that they will miss you by twenty yards; and all too often they seem to be satisfied with that. It does not seem to occur to those manning these ships that with your rough and ready calculations and judgements this seems like a collision course, and the scenario is prepared for the classic situation in which both vessels panic at the last moment and turn towards each other – as has happened all too often in recent years. A very early alteration on your part also will avoid this sort of situation developing, as well as obviating the risk of a sudden emergency as a large ship passes clear but very close – a steering breakdown perhaps.

Risk of Collision

It is a simple matter to determine if you are on a converging course with another vessel, in which case a 'risk of collision' is deemed to exist. You can see in figure 95 that if the relative bearing of the other vessel remains constant, or

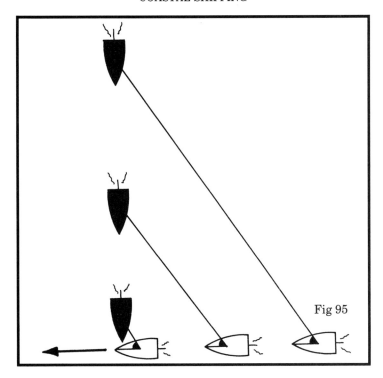

Fig 95

nearly so, the two of you will converge
and collide. Thus the first thing to do on
sighting another vessel that appears to
be closing is to take a relative bearing of
it. This should be repeated at intervals
to see if it remains steady. If it draws
ahead, so will the ship. If it draws astern,
so will the ship.

The safest way to take a relative
bearing, especially if you are yawing
about, is to take a compass bearing, then
maintain as steady a course as you can.
A simpler but less certain method is to
sight the vessel behind a stanchion or
stay and watch how it moves in relation
to it. Your course must be held steady
all the time, and your eye must remain
in the same place, or true relative bearings will not be obtained (see section on
Transits in chapter 8).

Taking Avoiding Action

If a risk of collision exists then you

must take action according to the rule
of the road, depending on whether you
are 'give-way vessel' or 'stand-on vessel'.
If the latter, then you should hold your
course and speed, so that the other will
know where you are heading. If the former, then as a general rule you should
alter course boldly to starboard and pass
under the other's stern. Do so in plenty
of time, so that he can clearly see what
action you are taking long before he has
cause for concern. This is invariably the
safest thing to do, and if everyone did it
there would be no collisions.

If a give-way vessel does not seem to
be taking sufficient avoiding action as
the two of you get close, then you should
do all you can to avoid a collision. Out at
sea, when there is a risk of no-one being
on watch on the other vessel, the only
safe thing to do is to alter course long
before a risk of collision exists (see above
section). In a close quarter situation it
is generally best to alter course hard

a-starboard as that is almost certainly what he will do when he wakes up and realises what is happening. The two of you will then pass clear of each other. Sound the requisite signals on your horn, as noted in appendix 2. A great many collisions are caused by vessels getting too close to each other, then the stand-on vessel panicking and altering to port just as the other alters to starboard. Both end up by turning towards each other and colliding.

Collision Avoidance with Radar

This is a risky business with small boats, generally caused by a combination of difficult working conditions, inadequate radar sets and inexperienced operators. The accuracy of the display on small yacht radars is not really up to collision avoidance at close quarters; it takes

Photo 24 (overleaf) *The behaviour of racing dinghy fleets can be very confusing, especially when they are working to windward. In a large vessel you are best to lean on the horn and go straight through the middle as this is likely to cause less trouble than if you try to avoid each and every one. At least they all then know what you intend doing! Often, however, you can spot a turning mark, like the buoy here in line with the yacht beyond, and this will help to make sense of where they are headed next.*

Photo 23 *The wake of a big ship passing very close at sea can interact with the existing waves and cause a brief but very disturbed sea (see chapter 7). In rough weather this is one more reason for keeping well clear of such shipping.*

skill and training to be able to use any radar safely for such a thing, especially in difficult conditions when many ships are converging (see chapters 10 and 14 for more detailed information on the reasons for this). Generally, radar on a small boat should be used for the purpose of keeping well clear of other shipping, long before a close quarters situation could develop.

Shipping Lanes

In certain places where large numbers of ships congregate, such as major headlands, turning points, and approaches to large commercial harbours, traffic is directed into 'lanes' going in opposite directions, much like cars on a road. These areas are known as Traffic Separation Schemes, and consist of two opposing lanes separated by an empty area called the Separation Zone, whose purpose is to keep ships on reciprocal courses well apart from one another. They are generally marked on charts (see figure 96). Usually there will be Inshore Zones, where small vessels can proceed along the coast without having to mix it with the big boys in the main shipping lane.

Full details of these separation schemes, and action to be taken by vessels in and near them, will be found in an Almanac, handbook or specialist Collision Regulations publication. Generally, shipping lanes should be crossed at right angles and as quickly as possible, and it should be borne in mind that large vessels in these lanes may be travelling at considerable speed, and may be hampered in their actions to various extents by the proximity of others, and by the requirements of the Collision Regulations with reference to vessels proceeding along shipping lanes. In a cross-stream it is your vessel's heading that should be maintained at right angles to the lanes, not the course made good. This makes it easier for others to judge your movement.

Strictly speaking, the normal rule of the road prevails in shipping lanes if a risk of collision develops. However, the rules state quite clearly that small vessels should navigate these areas in such a way as to prevent such a risk developing. In other words, keep out of their way long before a close quarters situation can develop. Sailing vessels without engines need to take particular care, especially in light winds, to judge the crossing of a shipping lane so as to get clear during a suitable gap in the traffic.

Even Inshore Traffic Zones are likely to be crowded at times with small vessels, especially around headlands and near the approaches to commercial harbours. Great care must be taken in all such areas.

Harbour Entry Channels

Major commercial harbours will have buoyed channels for the large ships, and these channels can be very busy at times. Almost certainly you will find sufficient depth of water outside the channel, and that is where you should safely remain. Many large harbours will designate suitable small boat routes, and these routes should be adhered to except when you have to cross a main channel. Very often the concentration of shipping can be such as to make it quite hazardous to cross these channels, and they should be treated as though they are shipping lanes. Cross as quickly as possible, keeping your heading at right angles to the flow of the traffic. Some harbours may designate suitable places for crossing, where the channel is narrow and where there is a good long view

Fig 96

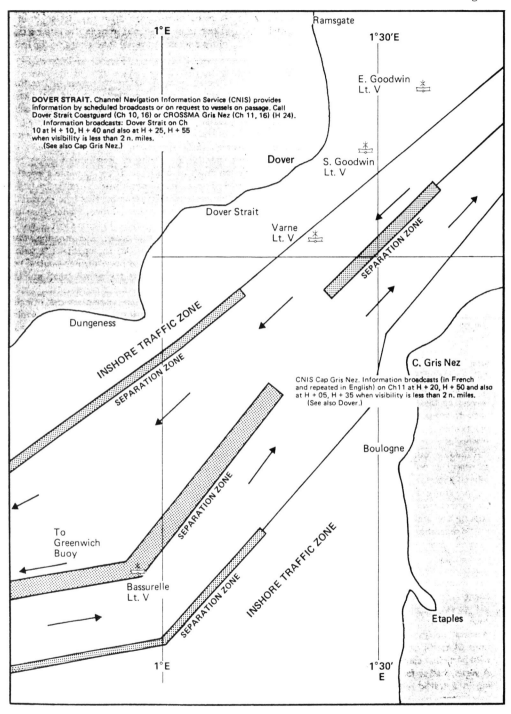

DOVER STRAIT. Channel Navigation Information Service (CNIS) provides information by scheduled broadcasts or on request to vessels on passage. Call Dover Strait Coastguard (Ch 10, 16) or CROSSMA Gris Nez (Ch 11, 16) (H 24).
Information broadcasts: Dover Strait on Ch 10 at H + 10, H + 40 and also at H + 25, H + 55 when visibility is less than 2 n. miles.
(See also Cap Gris Nez.)

Ramsgate

1°E

1°30′E

E. Goodwin Lt. V

Dover

S. Goodwin Lt. V

Dover Strait

Varne Lt. V

SEPARATION ZONE

INSHORE TRAFFIC ZONE

SEPARATION ZONE

Dungeness

C. Gris Nez

CNIS Cap Gris Nez. Information broadcasts (in French and repeated in English) on Ch11 at H + 20, H + 50 and also at H + 05, H + 35 when visibility is less than 2 n. miles.
(See also Dover.)

SEPARATION ZONE

Boulogne

To Greenwich Buoy

SEPARATION ZONE

Bassurelle Lt. V

SEPARATION ZONE

INSHORE TRAFFIC ZONE

Etaples

1°E

1°30′ E

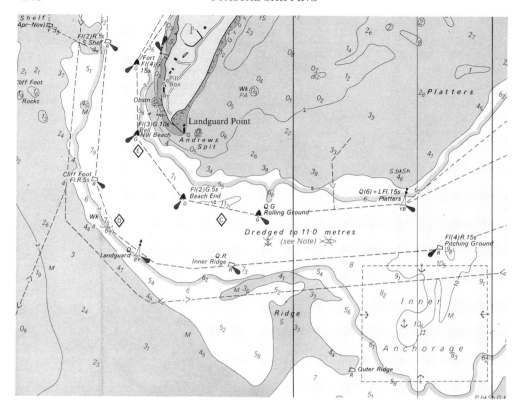

Fig 97 *To the north of the dredged channel you can see a pecked line with an arrow indicating the best crossing place for small craft. The yacht approach line can be seen south of the channel, marked with arrows in both directions. An approach route from the south-west to join this line is also marked at bottom left. This area is just to the west of that shown in figure 70.*

in both directions. Selecting a suitable spot such as this is particularly important for a sailing vessel without an engine, especially in light airs (see figure 97).

You must appreciate that ships in such channels do not have the manoeuvrability of those in shipping lanes. Also, unlike those in shipping lanes, they come under the category of vessels restricted in their ability to manoeuvre, and so have right of way over small boats, according to the rules. They may also travel surprisingly fast in these approach channels, not simply through being in a hurry to get home, but they may have a tide to catch into a dock, or they may need the speed to maintain steering control in such narrow waters. It simply is not safe for such vessels to alter course, stop or even just slow down in these circumstances, so you must keep well out of their way.

Fishing Vessels

Fishing vessels can pose particular problems as it is not always easy to figure out what they are doing, especially at night. The lights – if you can see them against the glare of decklights – will tell you whether he is or is not a trawler, which is not always as useful as it sounds. It is all very well to advise you to give all fishing boats a wide berth, but if you are approaching a large concentration of them this glib advice may well entail sailing thirty miles out of your way – which is not realistic.

Whatever the pretty lights shown in publications on lights and shapes, and the fact that sidelights should be displayed only when making way, and so on, you will find in practice that virtually all fishing boats switch on all their lights when they proceed to sea and turn them off when they tie up again. They also have so many powerful decklights for working by that it is almost impossible to see their identification lights anyway, except at dangerously close ranges. Daymarks are invariably fixed permanently in position, even in harbour, so that at any time it is rarely possible to ascertain whether a fishing boat is actually fishing, and requires right of way, or whether he is simply steaming and thus does not. Give them a good berth and let them get on with earning their living.

Trawlers

In general, trawlers can usually be passed quite close as their gear goes downwards fairly steeply from the stern, straight to the seabed. But when they are shooting or hauling their gear, the nets can lie on the surface quite a way astern of the trawler, and the boat is likely to make sudden, inexplicable alterations of course, or even steam round in circles. With the crew on deck in the glare of the working lights there is little chance of them seeing you, even in daylight if they are busy, and you must be very much on guard if circumstances cause you to be close when this

is happening. Trawlers tow very slowly – about 2 knots – and will appear to be virtually stationary when seen from a distance.

Pair trawlers tow a very large single net between two vessels, about ¼ mile abeam of each other. There should not be any problem passing between them should you have to, except when they are hauling. To do this the two vessels draw gradually together as the net is being winched in towards the surface, so it is not advisable to pass between them at this time! At night they may shine searchlights towards each other to indicate what they are doing.

Static Fishermen

The fishing vessel showing red over white is a rather more complex proposition. If he is hauling pots or longlines then he can be more or less treated as an anchored vessel, as his progress is minimal and the lines go almost vertically downward. However, if he is shooting the gear away, he may appear simply to be steaming on passage, but he will not be pleased if you try to cross ahead of him and cause him to mess up the direction in which he is laying his gear. So always pass well astern of a fishing vessel even if you think he is merely on passage and should thus avoid you.

Drift netters, lying to long lengths of net on the surface, should be given a very wide berth indeed if you have to pass to windward of them, as that is the direction the gear will lie, streamed from the bow and perhaps two miles long. Try to pass to leeward if you can. Sometimes, however, the nets are buoyed and the boat simply hangs about – usually at one end. It is then not easy to tell where the nets lie, although they are likely to be set across the tide. If you head for the boat, the clear passage will almost certainly lie close to one side of him; and he will undoubtedly let you know which side.

Angling vessels are not considered fishing vessels for purposes of the Collision Regulations, so do not require right of way. Often, though, they will drift on the tide with their lines out, and it would seem a courteous gesture to give them a clear berth if you can.

Seiners

These vessels work a bottom net very similar to a trawl, but they do not tow it along a set course as a trawler does. Instead, they shoot away and buoy one end, then steam slowly round in a large circle until they regain the buoy. Then they haul the net much as though they had been trawling. The fish is better quality than that caught by trawlers as it has not been dragged along in the cod end for three or four hours.

The big purse-seiner is the one type of fishing boat likely to display the optional lights described in the COLREGS, and if these are showing you should give such a vessel a very wide berth. Purse-seining consists of towing a huge surface net round in a vast circle to trap the fish, and it would not be wise to run into this net, as it probably cost the skipper some £50,000 or more and cannot be insured. Purse-seiners may behave rather erratically at times as it is not unknown for a huge shoal of trapped mackerel to suddenly start swimming off en masse, towing the ship behind them!

Warships

Generally these do not pose problems in the daytime as they are very manoeuvrable, and you can be fairly sure that an extremely good watch is being kept.

Look out, though, for sudden alterations of course and speed, and other strange behaviour, if they are carrying out manoeuvres. An aircraft carrier will display the lights and shapes for a vessel unable to manoeuvre, if it is flying off aircraft (see appendix 3). It will always steam straight into the wind at full speed (about 30 knots) when doing so, in order to assist the aircraft off the deck. A helicopter will be hanging around on rescue duty, and various frigates may be keeping station. Give the whole ensemble a wide berth.

You may come across warships replenishing at sea, also showing signals for being unable to manoeuvre, and the same comments apply. This is a tricky operation that takes some aligning and a fair bit of sea-room, so do not get in their way. If they are forced to break off and some sailor has to wait a few more hours for a letter from his girlfriend, he will not be very happy.

At night warships can be confusing to identify, as even the larger ones often have only one mast, and therefore only one steaming light. What appears to be a small yacht motoring along at 4 or 5 knots may turn out to be a 5,000-ton cruiser doing 35. The importance of checking the progress of approaching lights by taking bearings cannot be over-emphasised.

Submarines

Submarines occasionally get in the news for surfacing too close to small vessels, and for apparently getting caught in trawlers' nets. There are two basic problems with submarines, especially where sailing boats are concerned. The first is that it is extremely difficult for them to detect a quiet sailing boat when underwater, so there is always the chance that a periscope will pop up for a look round before he realises that you are there. The second is that the periscope is a very small, thin object that is virtually impossible to detect other than by its wake in flat calm water. It is also only a few feet high, so on its first initial sweep round to see what is about, he may well not spot a small boat in a lumpy sea.

A particularly good lookout must therefore be kept when passing through Submarine Exercise Areas (marked on charts) or in the approaches to submarine bases. This latter should be mentioned in Pilot Books. Even when on the surface submarines present a very low silhouette, thus making them distinctly inconspicuous at all but short ranges. They also carry their lights very low down at night, so giving the impression of being much smaller than they are.

Rule of the Road

In appendix 3 you will find potted information on the rule of the road. This is intended to serve as reference only. The full rules and details of lights and shapes shown by vessels will be found in specialist manuals and Almanac handbooks, and they should be studied thoroughly in those publications.

Pleasure Craft

It is not only commercial shipping and fishing vessels that cause problems to the coasting navigator; yachts and motorboats can also create difficulties, but usually for different reasons. The reason in these cases is generally amateurish incompetence or inexperience.

Windsurfers, speedboats and water scooters can be an absolute menace at times close inshore and in estuaries, as so many of the people playing with them cannot control the things. Neither do they usually have any idea whatever about rule of the road or other aspects of seamanship. The only real defences I can suggest are a loud horn, a fierce expression in conjunction with a large belaying pin, and to be poised for instant avoiding action in the expectation of moronic, irrational or incompetent behaviour.

Other Difficulties

There are a number of other problems that can face the coasting navigator, such as dredging operations, mine countermeasure exercises, firing ranges, submarine distress signals and so on. Useful information can be gained on these matters from the annual summary of Admiralty *Notices to Mariners* (available from a chart agent), local *Notices to Mariners* (pinned on noticeboards outside Harbour Offices), and from radio broadcasts by coastguards and coast radio stations (details in almanacs).

13
Making a Coastal Passage

Let us now see how to go about planning and making a coastal passage that involves pilotage rather than navigation, as most coastwise trips do for small boats.

Planning the Weather

Weather forecasts should be studied and recorded for some days beforehand, so as to get a clear picture of the way the weather is developing. If time is limited, you should be able to look ahead to the likely weather prevailing when you want to return, and then choose a harbour that will give you a good passage home. This is always more important than a good passage out; not only because you may have a job to return to, but also because psychologically the crew will be much less enthusiastic about a hard return passage than a hard outward one. At the same time, however, it is my experience that a short day trip followed by a night in harbour, and then a very early start, is preferable, at the beginning of a week's cruise, to bashing straight off into the wild blue yonder. Particularly with an inexperienced crew, it gives everyone a chance to find their sea-legs and settle down, before facing a long passage. It

is worth bearing in mind that even seasoned sailors will be rusty and out of sorts on the first cruise of the season, and this ploy reduces greatly the chance of seasickness.

Planning the Passage

Most coastal passages can be considered as three separate stages: getting out of the departure harbour and into a position from which course can be set to the destination; sailing to a convenient point outside the approaches to the destination; approaching and entering the destination harbour. The first and the third stages are pure pilotage, while the middle bit is likely to include dead reckoning and fixing in addition to pilotage techniques. The making of a coastal passage is much simplified by the separation of these three sections.

The initial stage of planning the passage consists of reading carefully the relevant Pilot Books for the areas, not only for detailed information on the harbours concerned, but also for tidal and other information appertaining to the actual passage. With this information absorbed into the mind, the charts should then be studied, paying particular attention to any dangers marked or noted. Follow your proposed route carefully along the chart and ensure that no dangers lie on or near it. The clearer a mental picture you can develop of the passage at this stage, the easier will be the last-minute plotting, and the actual carrying out of the trip when you might be cold, tired and seasick (see chapter 2).

You should also prepare rough plans, and have charts and Pilot Books for alternative harbours should the weather prevent you making the chosen one. Even if your chosen harbour is accessible in all conditions, you must consider the possibility of having to abandon it for other reasons – lack of time; seasickness or weariness in the crew; strong head winds, and so on.

The two most important factors involved in the detailed planning of a good passage under sail are: leaving at the right time; and going in the right direction; to both of which there is a good deal more than meets the eye. Let us consider the question of timing first.

Timing the Passage

Inevitably there will be certain places in a passage which are best negotiated at certain times, and perhaps some that *must* be negotiated at certain times. Planning a passage to accommodate all such considerations will rarely be possible, and compromise will have to be made. The first thing to do is to list all the parts of the passage that will be affected by timing, then sort them into priorities. The likely factors are:

1   Any limiting tidal height required for clearing the berth or leaving the harbour; because of a drying berth, marina sill, river bar, etc.

2   Any limiting times for leaving the harbour due to difficult or dangerous tidal streams, possible breaking seas on a bar, lack of shore lights dictating day-light, the need to see drying banks for navigation, and so on.

3   The need or desire (depending on level of risk) to pass through races, overfalls or narrow channels, or round headlands, etc, at a particular state of the tide.

4   The need or desire (as the case may be) to carry a fair tide along a coast, or lee-bow a tide across a channel, during certain stages of the passage.

5   The desire to cross busy shipping lanes in daylight.

6   The desire to make initial landfall at night, when coastal lights are visible for easy fixing.

7   The need or desire to approach and enter harbour in daylight, due to a difficult or unlit approach.

8   Tidal height or stream limitations on approaching and entering the destination harbour, as in 1, 2, and 3 above.

9   Whether a few hours' delay will allow the current weather pattern to change to a more favourable one; the passage of a cold front, for example, changing murky sou'westerly conditions into clear nor'westerly ones.

Working the Tides

All these factors notwithstanding, it is generally tidal streams that dictate the timing of an efficient coastal passage, especially under sail, and one often hears seasoned coastal navigators refer to 'working the tides'. In figure 98 you can see the sorts of benefits that accrue from a careful study of the tidal streams and the timing of a passage to make best use of them. In this situation the skipper endeavours to do the following:

1   Pass dangerous headlands (marked on the chart with rips, races or overfalls) at slack water.

2   Pass safe headlands with a fair

Photo 25 *If you berth in a marina with a half-tide cill like this one, you will be limited to when you can leave. The channel beyond dries right out and in order to improve the timing of later passage factors, it may pay you to leave on an early tide and get out to where you can anchor in deep water. You can then sail at a more convenient time for negotiating the rest of the passage.*

tide (as streams run strongest off headlands).

3 Sail into bays when the tide is foul. The stream will be much slacker in a bay, and there may even be a back eddy.

4 Cross shallow banks at High Water when the greater depth reduces the steepening and shortening effect of the shallow water on waves.

5 Cross river bars on the last of the flood, when the combination of extra depth and in-going stream reduces the likelihood of dangerous, breaking waves.

6 In strong onshore winds he will try to pass inside off-lying banks at Low Water so that they present the greatest possible barrier to the waves. The waves will then break on the bank and subside beyond it to give surprisingly calm waters inshore. If he can time this to coincide with lunch, all the better!

7 He will aim to negotiate very narrow passages with a weak foul tide as this will give him much more control over the boat than he will have with a sluicing tide under him. If necessary he can even slow right down while stem-

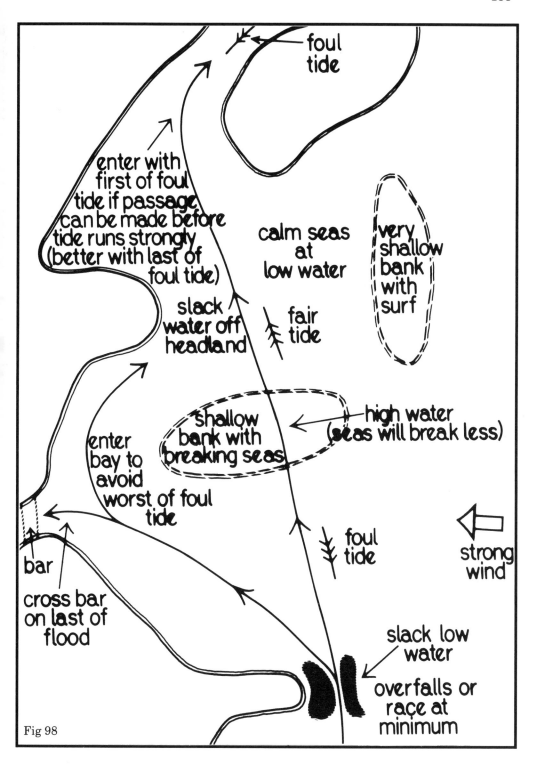

foul tide

enter with first of foul tide if passage can be made before tide runs strongly (better with last of foul tide)

calm seas at low water

very shallow bank with surf

slack water off headland

fair tide

shallow bank with breaking seas

high water (seas will break less)

enter bay to avoid worst of foul tide

bar

foul tide

strong wind

cross bar on last of flood

slack low water

overfalls or race at minimum

Fig 98

ming the tide, so as to actually remain stationary in relation to the ground. There may be times when this ability could be a life-saver.

Timing the Departure

There are a great many things here that must be considered before ever we decide on a suitable time to leave on the passage, and it is important to deal with them methodically if any sense is to be made of it all. The relative importance of the various factors must be compared, and the effects of alternative timings (such as leaving a drying berth on the flood or the next ebb) checked right through the passage. If, for example, you are limited to leaving a marina up to half tide but have no element of danger (such as a breaking bar) to contend with, you may find that staying in your cosy bunk for an extra three or four hours, till the ebb, may enable you to catch a fair tide round a troublesome headland, or lee-bow a channel tide before tacking towards a wind shift (see next section). On a simpler level, there is little point in flogging away to arrive off a small unlit port at midnight, then having to heave to till dawn, if you can stay in the pub for the evening and go off at first light on a twenty-four hour passage. Bearing in mind always, of course, the uncertainty of accurately timing any passage under sail. You do not want to arrive at a lock gate half an hour after it shuts, with a rising onshore gale and night falling.

Timing in Practice

If you can time this lot according to the plan, neatly turning everything to advantage all the way, then you must have influence in high places! The chances of timing everything just right are, of course, usually extremely remote

and, as ever, some compromise must be reached. In order to ensure passing dangerous headlands, etc, at suitable times you may have to accept bucking a foul tide along part of the coast. However, in suitable weather conditions there is no reason why you should not anchor while tides are foul, as they used to in the old days. If you are working to windward in a small or inefficient sailing boat there is a good chance that actually you will lose ground against a foul tide anyway, so there is a great deal to be said for ducking into a sheltered bay and lying peacefully to your anchor for a few hours over the strong half-tide period. You can all have a rest and a decent meal in comfort.

In many areas, though, you will be able to cheat a foul tide by standing into bays where slack water or back eddies exist, or by creeping along in the shallows where the tide is least strong (see chapter 4). Bear in mind, however, the possibility of cross tides flowing into bays and across banks that you might wish to sail over on the flood in search of slacker streams.

On some passages you may even find that you can fiddle more than six hours of fair tide by chasing the area of slack water where the tide is turning, as it moves along the coast. A careful study of the Tidal Stream Atlas will show whether this is possible at the speed you are sailing, and this is well worth trying to organise.

Setting the Course

If you have a fair wind to the destination, and it is forecast to remain fair for the duration of the passage, then all you have to do is calculate set and drift as described in chapter 5, then point the boat in the required direction, set the sails and put the kettle on. If the wind begins fair, but is forecast to shift ahead, then it might pay to set a course to one side of the destination so as to avoid having to beat when the wind shifts. This will require some thought, as it will not always be worthwhile. You will need to weigh up the extra time sailed against the time, effort and discomfort that might be saved by maintaining a free wind when it shifts. A few sums, some careful weather forecasting, and a little geometry will be required here. You should bear in mind that in a small boat there is generally a huge difference in speed and comfort, especially in fresh winds and a lumpy sea, between sailing hard on the wind and being cracked off even just a little to a close reach.

Headwinds

If the wind is inconsiderate enough to be on the nose at the start of the passage, and forecast to remain there, there are three basic ways of dealing with it. The first is to make just two long tacks; the second is to make a number of short tacks; and the third is to go somewhere else – you are cruising for pleasure, after all.

The first approach minimises the effort and delay caused by frequent tacking, as well as simplifying navigation, but it does entail the risk of overstanding the destination when tacking in from a long leg. If the wind shifts, there is also a risk of being caught dead downwind, just as you are about to stand in on the final leg, or of massively overstanding the destination if it frees you. If all goes well, however, it is quicker than short tacking.

The short tacking option removes the risk of overstanding and of being caught downwind in a shift, but does involve more navigation and greater accumulation of possible navigational

inaccuracies, as well as being slower in theory and more trouble generally. On the face of it the choice would seem to be a gamble on the risky efficiency of two long tacks or the slow and fiddly safety of a number of short tacks. The decision as to which approach to adopt is, however, frequently dictated by factors other than simple personal preference. Let us look at them.

The risk of overstanding the destination with two long tacks is greatly reduced by putting in the second tack early, producing in effect a passage of three tacks. With a steady wind forecast to maintain its direction, this is probably the best course, combining the advantages of both long and short tacking. It is particularly suitable for a small or weak crew, a boat that is slow in stays, or in rough seas when constant tacking is especially wearisome and time-consuming. If the wind is erratic, thus creating a danger of being caught downwind at the end of a tack, then the number of tacks can be gradually increased from the ideal of two until they produce a passage that takes the skipper no further from his direct track than he wishes to risk. The lengths of the tacks should be reduced gradually as the destination is approached, so that the boat remains within set angular limits of the destination (see figure 99 and the next section on tack limiting lines). This reduces considerably the risk of being caught downwind of the destination in a shift, and also of overstanding.

Windshifts

If the wind is forecast to shift to a particular direction during the passage, first a single long tack should be made towards the direction of the expected shift. Then when the shift comes, the boat will be strongly headed and can

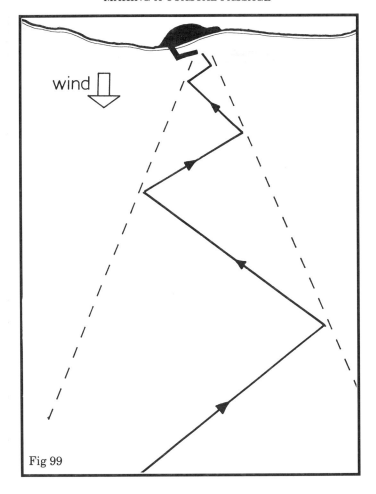

wind

Fig 99

tack immediately to take full advantage of the weather gauge that has now been gained. This technique needs careful judging as to the time of the expected shift, to prevent serious overstanding if it comes late. If you plot a limiting line back from the destination representing the course you can sail closehauled in the new wind, it will indicate how far you can sail safely away at any stage of the passage without the risk of overstanding when the wind shifts. If you then make your tacks (if more are needed to prevent overstanding) so as to keep between this line and the new

wind direction, you can be sure of a free wind when it comes (see figure 100).

Consider also the possibility of unforecast windshifts such as described in chapter 7. Standing inshore for a geographical shift or an early sea breeze may be beneficial, for example. Careful consideration and use of such factors can make huge differences to the efficiency and comfort of a passage.

Strong Winds

These can be quite a bugbear on a coastal passage, especially in fast tides.

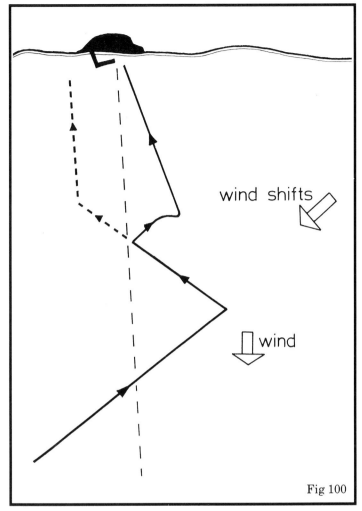

wind shifts

wind

Fig 100

If you are beating into a strong breeze, you want a fair tide to help you, but this will then be running against the wind and kicking up a rough sea. A lee-going tide will give noticeably calmer seas but likely will bring progress over the ground to almost zero. A useful ploy here, if the wind direction is suitable, is to stand into bays during the fair stream, so that the next headland will give some shelter from the seas. With luck you may be able to duck out of the worst of the waves without losing too much fair tide; it is the waves rather than the wind which slow you, when beating in rough weather.

You can then endeavour to dodge round the headland on slack water and creep right inshore on the next foul tide, to get both slack streams and calm seas. At the same time, however, you must avoid creeping close along a lee shore, for reasons stated in chapter 7.

Lee-bowing the Tide

If reasonably strong tidal streams are experienced from abeam or thereabouts during the passage, then by and large you should time your tacks so that the

Photo 26 *In the old days before engines these Thames trading barges would have anchored up in droves like this to await suitable fair tides or helpful slants of wind. Even today sailing vessels can profitably do the same thing when conditions conspire to make progress both slow and uncomfortable.*

tide is always setting up from leeward, underneath the lee bow. This is known as lee-bowing the tide and it has two benefits: it keeps the boat close to the direct track (in case of wind shifts); and it enables you to point higher and sail faster, due to the increase in apparent wind caused by the tide pushing you towards the wind (see figure 101). Nevertheless, normally it should not take priority over sailing towards a windshift – a free wind usually producing greater benefit than that gained by lee-bowing the tide. If the wind shift is expected late, initial tacks can profitably be set to take full advantage of lee-bowing effects before finally standing off towards the shift.

Huge savings in time and effort can be made if a passage is planned and executed according to these principles; and also by sailing a single course where possible, allowing the stream to carry you hither and thither, rather than constantly altering course to keep near the direct track to the destination (see chapter 5). The key to the whole thing is the weather; not one of these tactics is worth tuppence unless your weather forecasting is accurate, and I cannot stress too much the value of recording and studying a sequence of forecasts some days before setting off. It is the only way to get a real feel for the way the weather is developing.

Working the Weather

The experienced coastal navigator will not only work his tides to maximum advantage, but will also work his weather the same. If, for example, he is bound down the English Channel and there is a fresh sou'westerly blowing with attendant heavy rain, he will probably know from his weather forecasting that a frontal system is going through. A small mental calculation will then tell him that if he waits a few hours the cold front will pass over to give lighter nor'westerly winds and clear skies with good visibility. Not only will this enable a much pleasanter passage to be made, but he will probably arrive at his destination just as quickly as if he had spent those hours bashing into the sou'westerly.

If a succession of these frontal depressions is passing across the country and he wants to cruise the Channel for a week or so, with a little forethought he should be able to sail behind each cold front and spend his harbour time during the spells of bad weather ahead of each one. If he can then contrive to sail back east behind another cold front he will have a delightful passage with a fair wind in sheltered waters to round off an excellent sailing holiday in what

would otherwise seem to be a spell of bad weather. A similar approach can be adopted in the face of persistent radiation fog in an otherwise good spell of weather. All he has to do is sail between midday and late evening, and spend the foggy periods tucked up safe in harbour.

In calm, anticyclonic weather an engineless sailing boat can be sailed happily for days on end simply by putting to sea with the first of the sea breeze and mooring up late in the afternoon before it dies, leaving those who do not understand gasping and becalmed within sight of the cheerful harbourside pub!

On a longer term basis the skipper who can foresee and plan the weather will organise a cruise so that he finishes in a harbour upwind of home at the end of it – and so on.

This business of working the tides and working the weather is probably the real art of coastwise pilotage.

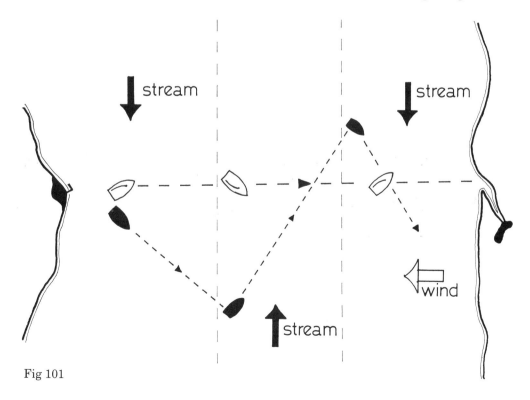

Fig 101

14
Piloting with Electronics

It is tempting to think, with the current proliferation of cheap and reliable electronic navigation aids, that traditional methods of position-fixing and navigation can be considered virtually extinct. It would be a foolish man indeed who did think so, for a variety of reasons. Even the manufacturers of these gadgets stress that they are no more than *aids* to navigation.

The Marine Environment

The first point to note is that all electrics and electronics are, by their very nature, susceptible to unreliability in a damp and salt-laden marine environment. However well protected your equipment may seem on perhaps a comfortable, dry, enclosed motor cruiser, cocooned in the warmth of the engine and ventilated by draughts of air, the moment you moor up and go back to work, so do the salt and damp.

These problems can be alleviated to a great extent by ensuring that all your electrical systems and electronic equipment are kept dry and well-ventilated at all times. Equipment should also be run as often as possible so that internal warmth generated by the components keeps the insides dry. Salt is the killer

rather than water, as even when the equipment is dried the salt remains and, being hygroscopic, will constantly absorb water from the atmosphere thus preventing the equipment from ever drying completely. Any electronic gear soaked in salt water should be thoroughly washed in fresh before being dried out.

Other sources of trouble, such as failing batteries, defunct alternators, poor electrical connections, vibration affecting badly-designed wiring runs, and so on, can all be contained by good initial design and construction followed by regular and thorough maintenance. It is impossible to stress this too much. Life on a boat is infinitely harder on equipment than is life in a motor car, and a failure at sea a great deal more than the mere irritation it is on land. As an engineer once said to me, you should mend things on a boat *before* they break.

All this applies to radars, echosounders, weatherfax machines, broadcast receivers, stereos, etc, just as much as to radio navigation systems.

Radio Navigation Systems

There are two basic types of system: those that give an absolute fix and those

that produce position lines. Satellite navigators and the ground-based hyperbolic systems such as Decca, Loran C and Omega come under the first category, while aids such as RDF, radio lighthouses, and so on, come under the second. There are important differences between these systems, which must be clearly understood. Those in the first group are generally extremely accurate and simple to use, and can provide a constant readout of the vessel's position without recourse to a dead reckoning plot or to navigation equipment other than a chart. Therein lie dangers which will be discussed later in the chapter. Equipment in the second group is, by and large, neither very accurate nor simple to use, and really can be utilised only in conjunction with a traditional DR plot and other tools. Position lines are produced which are simply plotted

Photo 27 *A modern yacht-type Decca Navigator giving a straight read-out of latitude and longitude. The buttons along the bottom provide many other facilities besides simple position, such as waypoint information, man-overboard marker and so on.*

like any other position line (see chapter 6).

Satnav

This works on very high frequency signals and gets its positional information from satellites orbiting the Earth. In essence, it measures the Doppler Effect of the changing frequency received as the satellite approaches. The current system, known as the transit system, uses four satellites in all and gets an actual fix about once an hour, as each satellite passes overhead. It requires course and speed information to be fed in so that it can compute a DR plot between fixes. This may be done automatically from electronic compasses and logs, or keyed in manually. A new proposed system for the 1990s, called GPS, will provide many more satellites, so producing fixes sufficiently frequently to avoid the necessity of dead reckoning between them. Accuracy depends on both the equipment and the quality of DR information fed in, but is typically somewhat better than ¼nm. Coverage is worldwide.

Decca

This is probably the most accurate of all radio navigators at present, giving a position in the best circumstances to within about 100 yards or even less. It is a hyperbolic, ground-based system that works by measuring the phase differences between low frequency signals received from various groups of master and slave transmitters. Signals from two pairs of transmitters (master and slave 1; and master and slave 2) will give two position lines, and thus a fix. Maximum range is about 400 miles from the master transmitter (250 at night), and present coverage is limited basically to Northern Europe as far south as Gibraltar.

Loran C

This works in the same basic way as Decca except that it measures time differences between the received signals instead of phase differences. This is a simpler system in a way, in that a time difference places the vessel immediately on a specific hyperbola, whereas the same phase difference could indicate a number of hyperbolae, the Decca receiver having to work out which one it is.

The low frequency of Loran C gives it a range of about 1,000 miles by day, and double this at night when it can utilise the sky wave (see later sections). It is not as accurate as Decca: about ¼ mile with the daytime ground wave, and maybe 2 miles on the sky wave at night. Coverage is limited to certain areas of the North Atlantic, North Pacific and Mediterranean, although this is likely to be extended in the near future.

Omega

This is far less accurate than Decca or Loran C but it has worldwide coverage. It works on the same basic principle but uses very low frequency signals, which bend round the globe to give the coverage. Accuracy is within about 1 mile in daytime and double this at night.

MF/DF

'Medium frequency direction finding' is often referred to simply as RDF (Radio Direction Finding). It measures the Magnetic compass bearing of special marine radio-beacons, and certain suitably-situated aero beacons. This bearing can be plotted from the beacon marked on the chart, in the same way as a visual compass bearing, and bearings from two or more beacons will provide a fix (see chapter 6). The comments made there about ranges and angular differences of visual bearings apply equally to RDF bearings. Working in a deviation-free place is also necessary for hand-held sets with built-in Magnetic compasses.

The bearing is obtained by tuning in to the frequency of the required beacon, identifying it by a Morse signal, then rotating an aerial until the continuous bearing signal disappears. Many of these stations are grouped together with the same frequency, and transmit in sequence so as to simplify the recording of bearings from a number of beacons. Full details of all this will be found in a nautical Almanac.

As well as being time-consuming and often difficult to use properly, MF/DF is riddled with errors and inaccuracies. A clear and precise 'null' point is often hard to obtain, thus producing a wide and woolly bearing. Rigging, guard-rails, metal masts, etc, can bend the bearing much as deviation does to a Magnetic compass. Bearings are affected by both ground and sky wave errors (see later sections). The bearing taken can be very difficult to judge when a boat is yawing in heavy seas.

Consol

This is a very simple system that requires only an ordinary broadcast receiver capable of tuning into the required frequencies, and fitted with a BFO (Beat Frequency Oscillator). It produces True bearings of special transmitting beacons by means of a series of dots and dashes that have only to be counted. By reference to special tables this count is converted into the bearing. It is long range (1,000 nm plus) but not very accurate, and really is of little use in pilotage work – it is also being phased out!

Radio Lighthouse

This is a new device similar to Consol in its mode of operation. However, it works through a normal VHF receiver to give much more accurate bearings at expected VHF ranges (about 20 miles), so is highly suited to coastal navigation. It is much easier to use and far more accurate and reliable than MF/DF as the bearing information is contained in the signal and does not have to be

judged from a perhaps wildly swinging compass. Being on VHF it is also not subject to all the propagation errors that affect MF/DF. At present only a few stations are in operation (see Almanac for details), but doubtless the system will grow.

VHF Radio Bearing

This is an emergency facility operated by many coastguard stations when requested by a call on VHF. Details are contained in the annual summary of *Notices to Mariners*.

Radio Range

This is a radio beacon signal, transmitted from some harbour entrances, that is designed for vessels to home in on. The term range here refers to a transit, not a distance. In principle one hears a continuous note when on track and different Morse signals when off to either side. The beam is like a lobe, starting wide and narrowing down until it fits through the harbour entrance, so there should be room for more than one vessel to follow it. This is not as silly as it sounds. There have been instances of fishing vessels following the same Decca lane in opposite directions and colliding, due to the precision of the system. This risk must be guarded against when using any sort of homing device.

Navtex

Although not a navigation aid, this is a useful electronic gadget that automatically receives messages about weather and sea conditions, localised dangers to shipping, shipping forecasts, and so on: the sort of information that is usually broadcast as SAYCURITAY messages by coast radio stations. Some present the information simply on a small screen, while others produce a printed readout. Weatherfax is a similar device that produces synoptic charts and shipping forecasts. Some fancy receivers incorporate both.

Inherent Defects

All these navigation systems utilise radio transmissions and there are two main problems that affect them. The first is the influence of land on the propagation of ground waves, and the second is the influence of the ionosphere on the propagation of sky waves. Ground waves are those that travel direct along the Earth's surface from transmitter to receiver, and sky waves are those that radiate upwards and are then reflected back to Earth by the ionosphere – a layer of electrically charged gases surrounding the Earth.

All ground-based medium and low frequency systems, such as Decca, Loran C, Omega and RDF are affected to varying degrees by inaccuracies caused by land interfering with the ground wave, and by the daily movement up and down of the ionosphere altering the reflection of sky waves. Satellite navigators are not influenced by either, as their very high frequency signals do not pass over land and are not refracted during their passage through the ionosphere. Neither are short range VHF or radio lighthouse bearings affected as they travel in a direct line from transmitter to receiver.

Ground Wave Effects

The basic problem here is that radio waves travel more slowly over land than they do over the sea. This has two distinct effects on the propagation of the waves. The first is that a radio wave that has travelled over land will arrive at the receiver later than a simple time, speed, distance calculation will forecast. This generates errors in systems that utilise timing or phasing of the waves for position fixing, such as Decca and Loran C. These errors are known as *fixed errors*, and they are normally listed in the equipment manual, for affected areas. They must be applied to the displayed position to get a true one.

The second type of error caused by the land is that of refraction. If a radio wave crosses a coastline at an angle, travelling slowly over the land beforehand, one end will clear the land, and thus speed up, before the other end. This causes the wave to bend, which generates at times considerable errors in systems utilising radio bearings for position finding, such as RDF (see figure 102). It does not affect hyperbolic systems as they are not dependent on bearings.

Sky Wave Effects

During the day the ionosphere, which is created by energy from the sun, is sufficiently dense for sky waves to be absorbed before they can be reflected to the ground. Thus the receiver picks up only the ground wave. At night the ionosphere thins out in the layers closest to the Earth. Sky waves reflected from the upper layers can then pass down freely to the ground and be picked up by the receiver. The distance from the receiver to this point, at which sky waves are received, is known as the 'skip distance'. As the receiver cannot distinguish between the ground and sky waves, it should be apparent that those depending on the travelling time of the waves – Decca and Loran C – become confused and can give spurious positions at ranges approaching the skip distance. Bearings from RDF stations

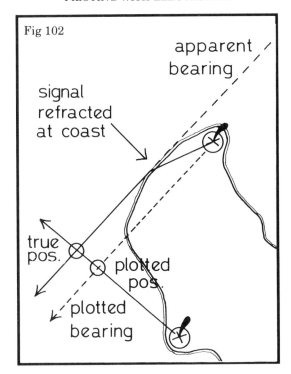

Fig 102

apparent
bearing

signal
refracted
at coast

true
pos.

plotted
pos.

plotted
bearing

also become distorted and inaccurate.

These errors are known as *random errors* as they cannot be accurately calculated, as can fixed ground errors. During the night, when the ionosphere has settled down, these errors are more reliable than they are during the dawn and dusk periods when the ionosphere is changing most rapidly. Their effects cannot be assessed for systems employing bearings – RDF, etc – so considerable errors can exist at ranges around and beyond the skip distance, particularly during the dawn and dusk periods.

Because of the nature of its signal, Loran C can distinguish between ground and sky waves, and thus can be set up to use the much greater range afforded by sky waves at night. Decca cannot distinguish between the two, so random errors are tabulated in a form indicating the maximum likely error that should be experienced at a particular time – night in winter, day in summer, etc.

Meteorological Effects

Snowstorms, thunderstorms and other meteorological disturbances can also affect the reception of radio signals, and their accuracy and reliability must be treated with caution in such conditions.

Radar

This is rather different in concept to the foregoing systems as it does not provide direct positions or position lines. Instead it presents on a screen a representation of what its scanner sees around the boat. This picture can then be used for fixing position in similar manner to a visual picture seen by the eyes. It can also be used for detecting and avoiding things such as ships and buoys.

However, as mentioned in chapter 10, it has considerable limitations compared to the human eye, and it is most important to understand these so that the equipment can be used intelligently, and not with blind dependence.

Signal Reflections

In general we can say that reflection is best from hard, metallic, vertical surfaces, and worst from soft, absorbent, sloping surfaces. From horizontal surfaces such as beaches and low jetties there may be no reflection at all. The coastline that shows so clearly on your screen may not be the line of coast drawn on the chart, but higher ground further inland. You need to check slopes

and heights of coastlines and inland mountain ranges very carefully before committing yourself to identifying the echoes on your screen.

The range obtainable by your set depends not only on its power, but also on the height of the scanner, as radar waves, like VHF signals, follow line of

Photo 28 *A top-quality, very high-definition radar set specifically designed for pilotage work. This is professional ship equipment and you can see the mass of very clear detail available to the pilot. Would that we could all have these on our small boats, but the size of both equipment and antenna preclude it.*

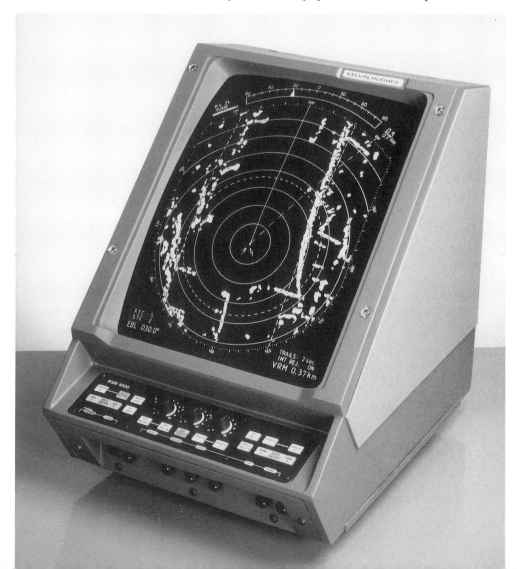

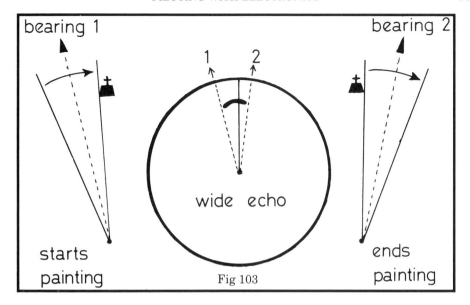

bearing 1

bearing 2

1   2

wide echo

starts
painting

ends
painting

Fig 103

sight. A 48-mile set on the deck of a small boat will give ranges around 5 miles (depending on height of target – see dipping range in chapters 6 and 8), not 48 miles. Occasionally, atmospheric conditions, such as temperature inversions, may cause the radar beam to bend over the horizon to give greatly increased ranges that may paint at spurious distances all over the screen, much like extra deep echoes on an echo-sounder. In certain places direct reflections from objects may interact with rebounds off the sea, to give blank areas with no reception. These are called Fresnel Zones (see Almanac for details).

Generally, however, you can reckon on 25-mile ranges for high cliffs, 3 miles for buoys with radar reflectors, and 1½ miles for withys (which show up surprisingly well), and pro rata for other objects. All these depend on meteorological and other conditions, so caution is required. A radar screen does not automatically show clearly everything the scanner looks at, like a television picture does.

Horizontal Beam Width

The horizontal beam width of a radar signal is by and large inversely proportional to the length of the scanner: the shorter the scanner, the wider the beam. Many small boat radars these days have very short (half-metre – 1ft 7in) scanners in order to reduce weight and windage aloft, and these can produce beam widths in excess of 5°, which is considered generally to be the minimum for a reasonably accurate picture.

The reason for this can be seen in figure 103. As the leading edge of the beam reaches a target, so the echo from that target begins to paint on the screen. It will then continue to paint until the trailing edge of the beam finally clears it. Thus a wide beam will produce a wide echo from even a small target such as a buoy. A bearing taken of this echo will be highly inaccurate as you cannot be certain precisely which part of the paint is the true position of the target. In general, ranges taken from a radar screen will be fairly accurate, as long as the target is identified correctly (see above). Bearings, however, unless the beam width is very narrow (Naval radars may have widths as little as ½°) will be very suspect and should be avoided if at all possible. The best type of radar fix is obtained from the intersection of three or more ranges.

A further problem caused by wide beams is that two small objects close together may paint as a single target, due to the beam picking up the second before losing the first. Channel buoys, narrow harbour entrances, etc, can suffer from this trouble. As you close the range, however, so the actual width of the beam will narrow and these objects will separate out into individual echoes.

Radar Beacons

Known as Racons, these are special transponders that detect the emissions from your radar set and transmit signals in reply. This signal shows on your screen as a line extending from a point slightly beyond the transponder's position towards the centre of the display. These lines generally include a Morse identification signal. Racon equipped navigation marks will be indicated on the chart by means of a special mark (see *Chart Booklet 5011* or Almanacs for details).

Racon signals can be erratic at times, and they should only be relied upon when you are within their normal range (ten miles or so) and the signal on your screen is regular and consistent. In conditions of abnormal radio wave propagation they can produce signals from far beyond the quoted range, and these signals can appear at random distances along the bearing of the racon. Racons may also be discontinued without warning, for maintenance, etc.

Using Electronic Navigators

Clearly, for all their limitations, I am not advocating the abolition of electronic navigators. There can be few old sailors who would not have given their eye teeth at times for a small black box, barely large enough to hold a dozen cigars, that could give them a continuous readout of their position to within about 200 yards, twenty-four hours a day, 365 days a year, in all weathers.

The real danger, however, is that regular use of such a device must inevitably take away from a navigator that delicate sense of how the elements are affecting his boat's progress, the accumulated knowledge of the way in which his boat responds to particular wind and sea conditions, and his essentially defensive approach to navigation. By the last I mean an innate antipathy to getting into a situation from which he cannot reliably extricate himself if all goes wrong.

Many of the traditional techniques discussed in this book are based on keeping out of danger rather than actually calculating a precise position. This approach to the task is what might be termed 'failsafe', in that however inaccurate the navigation may be, whatever miscalculations the navigator may make, and whatever unexpected horrors may befall him, he can always keep his vessel in safe water. This is very much the essence of good pilotage, and good seamanship.

If a navigator works entirely from his black box, allowing it to make cross-track error calculations for him, tell him the course to steer to a waypoint and so on, he must surely lose his feel for the boat. He must surely lose the ability to stand on deck quietly for five minutes and assess with tolerable accuracy his leeway, his helmsman's error and his speed. If, however, he simply uses the positional information given as though it were a fix, in conjunction with a traditional dead reckoning plot, and always approaches pilotage problems as though he had nothing other than a compass, a leadline and a biscuit (Dutchman's Log!) to guide him, the machine will be worth a place by the chart table.

For pilotage work Decca is the most accurate system, closely followed by Loran C. The area of coverage will probably dictate the one you use. The two worldwide systems – Omega and Satnav – are better suited to offshore navigation.

The field of electronic navigation is currently in a state of flux, due to the rapid development of new systems. Before investing in a radio navigator you should study the latest information which can be found in the yachting magazines.

Radar and the position line systems do not create the same psychological problems as the radio navigators, but they must still be used with caution and not be totally relied upon. They constitute merely additional weapons in the overall armoury of the navigator, and like any weapons they must be used with skill and experience if they are to work efficiently. The same comment may be applied to everything else in this book.

Buoyage Systems

IALA (International)

Lateral Marks – marking sides of a channel
(in relation to main flood tide or as indicated on chart by ⌂)

Port Side of Channel
: red can buoy
: red home-made buoy (beer barrel, etc)
: red beacon
: withy showing red (paint; red tin on top, etc)
: anything showing can-shaped topmark
: red light showing any type of rhythm
: buoys with even numbers painted on them

Starboard Side of Channel
: green conical buoy
: green home-made buoy (beer barrel, etc)
: green beacon
: withy showing green (paint; green tin on top, etc)
: anything showing conical topmark
: green light showing any type of rhythm
: buoys with odd numbers painted on them

Cardinal Marks – indicate direction of safe water: see diagram

All marks are coloured in black and yellow horizontal bands and have black topmarks. Black topmarks point towards black bands.

North of Danger
: topmarks point up (north)
: black band at top (north)
: light flashes continuously

East of Danger
: topmarks point outwards (like Greek E)
: black bands outside yellow band (where topmarks point)
: light flashes in groups of three (three o'clock)

South of Danger
: topmarks point down (south)
: black band at bottom (south)
: light flashes in groups of six (six o'clock)

West of Danger
: topmarks point inwards (like W on its side)
: black band in middle (where topmarks point)
: light flashes in groups of nine (nine o'clock)

Isolated Danger Marks are black, red, black with black topmarks
Safe Water Marks are white and red with red topmarks
Special Marks are yellow with yellow topmarks

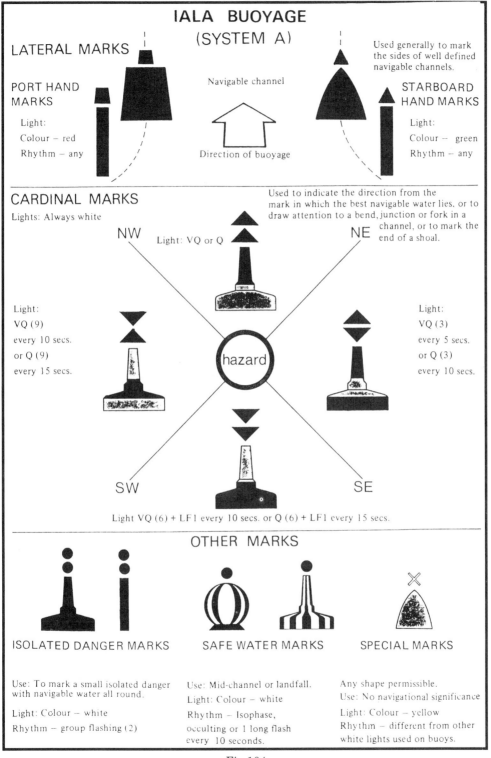

IALA BUOYAGE
(SYSTEM A)

LATERAL MARKS

Navigable channel

Used generally to mark the sides of well defined navigable channels.

PORT HAND MARKS

Light:
Colour – red
Rhythm – any

Direction of buoyage

STARBOARD HAND MARKS

Light:
Colour – green
Rhythm – any

CARDINAL MARKS

Used to indicate the direction from the mark in which the best navigable water lies, or to draw attention to a bend, junction or fork in a channel, or to mark the end of a shoal.

Lights: Always white

NW   Light: VQ or Q   NE

Light:
VQ (9)
every 10 secs.
or Q (9)
every 15 secs.

hazard

Light:
VQ (3)
every 5 secs.
or Q (3)
every 10 secs.

SW   SE

Light VQ (6) + LF1 every 10 secs. or Q (6) + LF1 every 15 secs.

OTHER MARKS

ISOLATED DANGER MARKS   SAFE WATER MARKS   SPECIAL MARKS

Use: To mark a small isolated danger with navigable water all round.

Light: Colour – white
Rhythm – group flashing (2)

Use: Mid-channel or landfall.
Light: Colour – white
Rhythm – Isophase, occulting or 1 long flash every 10 seconds.

Any shape permissible.
Use: No navigational significance
Light: Colour – yellow
Rhythm – different from other white lights used on buoys.

Fig 104

USWMS (American waterways)

Lateral Marks

Upstream is towards the head of navigation unless otherwise stated. Shapes of buoys may vary but colour does not. Numbers are white; they increase as you head upstream. Lights may be flashing, occulting or isophase. Rhythms are normally slow (<30/min); but quick (>60/min) at obstructions, bends, etc.

Cardinal Marks

Lights are quick flashing to denote bend, obstruction, etc.

Regulatory Markers

White with international orange stripes.

International orange shapes in centre give information, warning, etc.

Rectangle = information (directions; fuel; stores, etc)

Diamond = danger (rock; submerged cable; dam, etc)

Diamond & Cross = boats keep out; may give reason under (as shown)

Circle = controlled area (no ski; no swim; fishing only, etc)

General Information

Lights, reflectors, numbers and letters are discretionary. Letters may be used on regulatory and obstruction markers, in alphabetical sequence heading upstream (I and O not used).

IALA (System B)

It should be apparent that the colours of the USWMS lateral marks could be very confusing if encountered in conjunction with those of the IALA System A. To remove this confusion IALA System B is used instead in those countries where existing systems might conflict with lateral buoyage colouring. These countries are North and South America and Japan.

IALA System B is identical in all respects with System A except that port-hand lateral marks are green with green lights (instead of red), and starboard-hand lateral marks are red with red lights (instead of green).

UNIFORM STATE WATERWAY MARKING SYSTEM (USWMS)

LATERAL MARKS

Used to mark sides of
well-defined channels
and narrow waterways.

Navigable channel

PORT HAND
MARKS

Numbers - odd
Color - black
Light - Fl. G
Reflecter - green

Heading upstream

STARBOARD
HAND MARKS

Numbers - even
Color - red
Light - Fl. R
Reflecter - red

CARDINAL MARKS

Used where no clear channel
exists, or where obstruction
may be approached from
more than one direction.

Pass to North or East of mark.

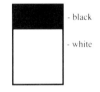

- black

- white

Light - white, quick flashing
Reflecter - white

↖NW

DANGER

SW ◁

red -

white -

Light - white, quick flashing
Reflecter - white

Pass to South or West of mark.

OTHER MARKS

Thin red
stripes
on white

Do not pass between
buoy and shore
Light - white, quick flashing
Reflecter - white

Blue stripe on white
Light - slow flashing or
quick flashing if buoy
is an obstruction.

OBSTRUCTION MARK

MOORING BUOY

STATE REGULATORY MARKERS - all orange and white

Marks in
centre

➡

BASS RIVER
FUEL

ROCK

SWIM ◇ AREA

5
MPH

BUOY/BEACON   INFORMATION   DANGER   KEEP CLEAR   CONTROL

Fig 105

Important Signals

Phonetic Alphabet and Morse Code

A	ALPHA	· —
B	BRAVO	— · · ·
C	CHARLIE	— · — ·
D	DELTA	— · ·
E	ECHO	·
F	FOXTROT	· · — ·
G	GOLF	— — ·
H	HOTEL	· · · ·
I	INDIA	· ·
J	JULIET	· — — —
K	KILO	— · —
L	LIMA	· — · ·
M	MIKE	— —
N	NOVEMBER	— ·
O	OSCAR	— — —
P	PAPA	· — — ·
Q	QUEBEC	— — · —
R	ROMEO	· — ·
S	SIERRA	· · ·
T	TANGO	—
U	UNIFORM	· · —
V	VICTOR	· · · —
W	WHISKY	· — —
X	X-RAY	— · · —
Y	YANKEE	— · — —
Z	ZULU	— — · ·

(Use to spell out callsigns and difficult or foreign words)

International Code – Single Letter Signals

A I have a diver down – keep clear

B I am loading, unloading or carrying dangerous cargo

C Yes; affirmative

D* Keep clear of me, I am manoeuvring with difficulty

E* I am altering course to starboard

F I am disabled – communicate with me

G I require a pilot – OR – I am hauling nets

H* I have a pilot on board

I* I am altering course to port

J I am on fire with dangerous cargo – keep clear

K I wish to communicate with you

L You should stop your vessel instantly

M My vessel is stopped and making no way

N No; negative

O Man overboard

P Vessel is about to sail – OR – my nets are caught on the bottom

Q My vessel is healthy and I require free pratique

R* – (no meaning except by sound in fog – see Fog Signals) –

S* My engines are going astern

T* Keep clear, I am engaged in pair trawling

U   You are standing into danger
V   I require assistance
W   I require medical assistance
X   Stop what you are doing and watch
     for my signals
Y   I am dragging my anchor
Z   I require a tug – OR – I am
     shooting nets

(Use International code flag; or Morse
code light; or Morse code sound)
(* = use sound only as Fog Signal or
Manoeuvring Signal [see below])

Fog Signals

Power vessel under way:
    – sounds 1 long blast every 2 minutes
Power vessel stopped:
    – sounds 2 long blasts every 2 minutes
Sailing vessel:
Fishing vessel:

Danger Signals

The following signals (from lightship,
coastguard, etc) mean:
    – 'You are standing into danger'.

Code flag U
Code flags N above F
U in Morse by light or sound
Gun or white flare
Rocket sound signal showing white
stars
Explosive sound signal repeated
Code flags P above S (by lightship means
'Do not come closer')
Towing vessel:
Vessel not under command:
Vessel restricted in manoeuvrability:
    – sounds Morse code D (— · ·) every
2 minutes
Vessel being towed (if manned):
    – sounds Morse code B (— · · ·) every
2 minutes
    – (immediately after tug's signal)

Vessel at anchor:
    – 5 seconds ringing of a bell for'ard
every 1 minute
    – followed by 5 seconds on a gong aft
(vessels over 100 metres)
    – may sound Morse code R (· — ·) to
warn approaching vessel
Vessel aground:
    – 3 strokes on bell; then anchor signal;
then 3 strokes on bell
Pilot vessels:
    – suitable signal from above list
    – may also sound Morse code H (· · · ·)

(On hearing fog signal ahead – sound
yours immediately after)

Manoeuvring Signals

I am altering course to STARBOARD –
    1 short blast (·)
I am altering course to PORT – 2 short
    blasts (· ·)
My engines are running ASTERN – 3
    short blasts (· · ·)
Are you taking enough avoiding action?
    – 5 short blasts (· · · · ·)
I intend to OVERTAKE you: – 2 long
    blasts (— —)
        followed by:
        on your STARBOARD side – 1 short
blast (— — ·)
        on your PORT side – 2 short blasts
(— — · ·)
I agree to be OVERTAKEN – Morse
    code C (— · — ·)
I am approaching a bend in the channel
    – 1 long blast (—)

(Use only when vessels are in sight of
one another)

Short blast = 1 second
Long blast = 5 seconds

3 short blasts does not imply the vessel
is actually moving astern

(Note use of Morse signals with suitable International code meanings)

Port Traffic Signals

These are often in evidence at busy commercial harbours, locks and bridges, and they vary from place to place. Full details will be found in the local Pilot Book. An attempt is being made gradually to standardise these signals, and those shown opposite will eventually be the standard International Port Traffic Signals.

Colours of lights are as follows:

Signals 1 and 2	– all lights RED
Signal 3	– all lights GREEN
Signal 4	– GREEN, GREEN, WHITE (from top)
Signal 5	– GREEN, WHITE, GREEN
Signals 2a and 5a	– see Note 4

INTERNATIONAL PORT TRAFFIC SIGNALS

No	Lights	Main message
1	 *Flashing* (three flashing lights, vertical)	Serious emergency – all vessels to stop or divert according to instructions
2	 (three lights, vertical)	Vessels shall not proceed (*Note*: Some ports may use an exemption signal, as in 2a below)
3	(three lights, vertical)	Vessels may proceed. One way traffic
4	(three lights, vertical, bottom white)	Vessels may proceed. Two way traffic
5	(three lights, vertical, middle white)	A vessel may proceed only when she has received specific orders to do so (*Note*: Some ports may use an exemption signal, as in 5a below)
	Exemption signals and messages	
2a	 *Fixed or Slow Occulting* (two columns: left three lights, right top light)	Vessels shall not proceed, except that vessels which navigate outside the main channel need not comply with the main message
5a	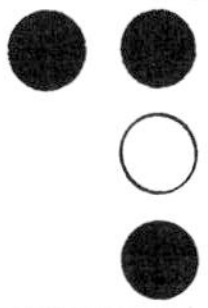 (two columns: left four lights with third white, right top light)	A vessel may proceed only when she has received specific orders to do so, except that vessels which navigate outside the main channel need not comply with the main message
	Auxiliary signals and messages	
	White and/or yellow lights, displayed to the right of the main lights	Local meanings, as promulgated in local port orders

Fixed or Slow Occulting (column label for Nos 2–5)

This new system is gradually being introduced, but its general adoption is likely to take many years.

Notes on use:

(1)   The main movement message given by a port traffic signal shall always comprise three lights, disposed vertically. No additional light shall be added to the column carrying the main message. (The fact that the main message always consists of three vertical lights allows the mariner to recognise it as a traffic signal, and not lights of navigational significance). The signals may also be used to control traffic at locks and bridges.

(2)   Red lights indicate 'Do not proceed'.

(3)   Green lights indicate 'Proceed, subject to the conditions stipulated'.
    (For examples, see opposite).
  Note that, to avoid confusion, red and green lights are never displayed together.

(4)   A single yellow light, displayed to the left of the column carrying main messages Nos 2 or 5, at the level of the upper light, may be used to indicate that 'Vessels which can safely navigate outside the main channel need not comply with the main message'. This signal is of obvious significance to yachtsmen.

(5)   Signals which are auxiliary to the main message may be devised by local authorities. Such auxiliary signals should employ only white and/or yellow lights, and should be displayed to the right of the column carrying the main message. Ports with complex entrances and much traffic may need many auxiliary signals, which will have to be documented; but smaller harbours with less traffic may only need one or two of the basic signals, such as 'Vessels shall not proceed' and 'Vessels may proceed, two way traffic'.
  Some signals may be omni-directional – exhibited to all vessels simultaneously: others must be directional, and be shown either to vessels entering or to vessels leaving harbour.
  Signal No 5 is based on the assumption that some other means of communication such as VHF radio, signal lamp, loud hailer, or auxiliary signal will be used to inform a vessel that she may specifically proceed.
  The 'Serious Emergency' signal must be flashing, at least 60 flashes per minute. All other signals must be either fixed or slow occulting (the latter useful when background glare is a problem). A mixture of fixed and occulting lights must not be used.

Fig 106

Rule of the Road Summary

Basic Rule of the Road

Sailing vessel meeting another:
– port tack keeps clear of starboard tack
– windward vessel keeps clear of lee-ward vessel (on same tack)
– overtaking vessel keeps clear

Sailing vessels keep clear of:
– vessels they are overtaking
– vessels fishing
– vessels not under command
– vessels restricted in manoeuvrability
– vessels constrained by draught

Power vessel meeting another:
– keeps clear of vessels on starboard side
– if closing head on, both alter clear to starboard
– overtaking vessel keeps clear

Power vessels keep clear of:
– all other vessels

For a full discussion of this extremely important aspect of coastal sailing see my book *Rules of the Road* (Fernhurst Books).

Index

page numbers in italics refer to illustrations or captions